3-2-61
7-6-60

The Christian, The State, and the New Testament

By

ARCHIE PENNER

1959

HERALD PRESS

SCOTTDALE, PENNSYLVANIA

Preface

In presenting this book to the reading public, the author is fully aware of the fact that its thesis is and has been a most perplexing one in the areas of Christian theology and ethics. Many and better minds have grappled with the problems for which an understanding and some answers have been sought in the following pages. However, the author feels that this book should make some contribution in its field of research and thought. It is at least with this purpose in mind that the book has been submitted to its publishers. The readers will have to judge in how far this purpose has been accomplished.

It is no doubt true, as has often been stated, that there is a greater tendency in the area of religious or theological concepts than in some others to be subject to emotional influence. This is understandable since the deeper dimensions of the human personality are undoubtedly more strongly involved. Experience has shown that this is even more true concerning the subject discussed in this book because the doctrine of nonresistant love with all of its implications and exacting demands cannot be squared with a pragmatically conditioned approach to the problems of human society. As a result, some of the assumptions and many of the conclusions are the most difficult to accept from the standpoint of what is humanly acceptable. This being so, the author has tried sincerely to be objective in determining the truth about the abiding problems of the Christian's relation to the state. He takes the view that the Scriptures must be determinative of what must be accepted or rejected as ethically binding upon the Christian.

As a consequence, he has desired above all else to be faithful to the Word, regardless how difficult the practical application of its truth may be. The total question is not: "What can I do?" or "What would I do?" but "What must I do?" under this or that circumstance.

The author wants to express his deep indebtedness to so many who have had an influence in making this book possible. It is not possible to name them all. Drs. H. S. Bender, J. C. Wenger and Guy F. Hershberger, all of Goshen College and Seminary, must be specially mentioned. The understanding and objective considerations which the thesis committee—Drs. E. Cairns, chairman, M. C. Tenney and R. Kamm, all of Wheaton College—showed, has been greatly appreciated and valued.

Most of the material in this book was originally gathered and written as a thesis under their guidance and presented to Wheaton College as a partial fulfillment of requirement for the M.A. degree. Their kind permission to publish the material in this form has been gratefully accepted. The close association with the faculty of the Steinbach Bible Institute and the help they have rendered in reading the manuscript must not go unmentioned. Then, too, the labours which my constant and understanding "helpmeet," Elvira, has devoted to accomplish the task, cannot be rewarded sufficiently.

The Christian helpfulness of both publishing houses has been no small matter in making the book what it is.

And so with much gratefulness and prayer that Christ will be honoured and His Kingdom enhanced and built, this volume is sent forth.

Archie Penner.

Steinbach, Manitoba, Canada.
May 21, 1959.

Introduction

The author of this compact and clearly written study is right in insisting that the problem of the Christian relation to the state has become a serious and important one in our time. Major problems of theology and ethics are involved—God's sovereignty, man's loyalty and obedience, the role and function of the state, the meaning of Christian love. He is right also in insisting that the Christian must seek the answer to these problems in the teachings of the New Testament, not in the Old Testament or in the history of the Church. He modestly indicates that he cannot present a complete guide for the details of the modern Christian's conduct in his relations with the state, since the New Testament itself does not do this; but he does confidently draw some general conclusions setting forth the main principles. I find his results fully satisfying.

This is essentially a study in New Testament theology. As such it follows sound principles of interpretation and theological method, presenting separately the teachings of Jesus, Paul, Peter, and John. It is an honest study, and completely loyal to the Scriptures. It is a pleasure to read a book which combines good exegesis, good theology and clear writing on an important contemporary subject.

The author is fully committed to the historic Anabaptist-Mennonite position, but he has nevertheless delivered an objective study, one which has much to say to those not in this tradition who seek to know and do the will of God in regard to the Christian's relation to the state. Such are invited to a careful examination of the author's results. Many Mennonites also need this practical and convincing treatise.

I heartily recommend this work to what I am confident will be a wide and appreciative audience. In the gradually increasing list of good books and booklets by Mennonites in the related subjects of war, peace, nonresistance, the state, and the Christian ethic of love, it will fill a place occupied by no other and its publication is accordingly fully justified. I am happy that it can appear as a joint issue by Mennonite publishers from both Canada and the United States. It is a token of solidarity across the border.

Goshen, Indiana.   Harold S. Bender.

CONTENTS

CHAPTER I

INTRODUCTION

A Question for Christendom

When one reviews the history of the persecution of the early Christians, also of the Anabaptists and Mennonites, and the continued conflict between them and the state, one is driven to an examination of the validity of the Biblical views they have held.

Pacifists, and conscientious objectors, especially in an emotional hour of national crises such as war, are often unpopular. They have been called cowards, sentimentalists and anarchists.[1] They even have been considered unbalanced and have been reminded that "True Christian Churchmen are dying for Christ."[2] Again, the conscientious objector was referred to "as 'a man who uses his religion to cloak a yellow streak.' "[3] A bishop once advised, " 'Let him be deprived forever of all benefits of war, of all political and social and civil rights.' "[4] Severe as these charges are, the extreme of irresponsibility was reached in derogatory remarks concerning the pacifist when Billy Sunday suggested that the pacifist was unfit to live in society. Sunday "is reported to have said 'The Christian Pacifists ought to be treated as Frank Little was at Butte and then let the coroner do the rest.' "[5] These quotations show what characterizes much of the thinking concerning the pacifist and the conscientious objector.

Indeed, the world at large, from Celsus[6] to Reinhold Niebuhr[7], including many professed Christians, has looked upon the pacifist and nonresistant Christian with more or less scorn. Not only has he been charged with causing the ruin of the Roman Empire but also with being a parasite on the sins of society. With this type of sentiment prevalent and often finding expression during World War II, the author, being a Canadian and a nonresistant Christian but being called to military service under the conscription laws of Canada, did not find it easy to withstand the pressures against his nonresistant conviction. These facts fully justify a re-examination of the whole area of the Christian's relation to the state.

The Mennonite church itself needs to re-examine its views on this subject. The reasons for this are numerous. The Mennonite church is obliged to re-examine its position continually, because of the far-reaching effects of its relations to the state and because of great social changes. There is also the possibility of error in the exegesis of any Bible doctrine. Another reason for re-examination, which stands out boldly, is the record of drafted men among the Mennonites in North America in World War II.

A Mennonite Central Committee draft census showed that of all the groups of Mennonites in the United States, as of December 1, 1944, 45.9 per cent went into CPS (Civilian Public Service), 14.5 per cent went into noncombatant military service, and 39.6 per cent took regular military service.[8]

In the largest group—the Mennonite Church—60 per cent of the men inducted were CPS men, 10 per cent were noncombatant, and 29 per cent were in the regular service. The General Conference Mennonites had over 27 per cent in CPS, 18 per cent were noncombatant, and over 54 per cent went into regular military service. The Mennonite Brethren had 39 per cent of their drafted men in CPS, 26 per cent went as noncombatants, and 34 per cent went into military service.[9]

These statistics suggest that Mennonites succumbed to social pressures without changing their basic concepts, or they deviated from the basic belief in nonresistance. The latter conclusion, with some allowance for the former, is perhaps the soundest. If this is correct, a need for a thorough re-examination of the effectiveness of the church's teaching program and its view of the relations of the Christian to the state is essential.

The Contemporary Conscience and War

Amid the world-shaking events of the past half century, there has been a new emergence in the thinking of the western mind on the moral justification of war. For many thinkers the problem of wars in recent years has pointed to the conclusion that man is inevitably a sinner—ineradicably evil.[10] The sinfulness of war is here clearly assumed.

Further light on recent Christian thinking concerning war and its evil are well described by Paul Hutchinson. He says,

For the Christian church, this problem of its relationship to the necessarily totalitarian war-making state has attained a new tension because the church is plagued by the moral problem of war as it never has been before.

*   *   *

There was, moreover, a widespread demand that the churches should bear their part in the national war effort, 'repentantly,' and church resolutions called forth by the war were peppered with that term. To fight repentantly, in most cases, meant no more than to fight sorrowfully, to fight regretfully, to fight remorsefully. This, it hardly needs to be pointed out, is to prostitute a great word in the vocabulary of religion. There can be no true repentance without a faithful effort to turn away from the sin of the past and to commit it no more.[11]

Another writer points up the problem of war and the Christian church when he reminds the Protestants that their churches, in World War I have given a "most recent striking occasion of almost universal spiritual endorsement of the State policies of violence, systematic falsehood, and wholesale violations of the rights of private conscience."[12]

Emil Brunner, the contemporary Swiss theologian, discusses the problem of war and the Christian ethic. He shows that

11

the present problem calls for new measures. He reveals his idea of the intenseness of the new problem by suggesting that "a new form of the State seems to be the need of the moment; the old form of parliamentary government . . . has come to an end of itself just as medieval feudalism [did] . . ."[13] One may not agree with Brunner's thesis, but it does point up the problem. The problem of war and the Christian is clearly a problem between the Christian and the state.

Perhaps another reason for a new emergence of the subject in recent times is the fact of the modern totalitarian state. The totalitarian state is not new. The modern democracies which western civilization seems to have taken for granted as a natural outcome of the evolutionary process are new.[14] When the holocaust of war was upon western civilization its eyes were opened. It saw the evil of the totalitarian state. It also saw the totalitarian element in all statehood. A few writers have pointed up this trend.

Christopher Dawson, speaking of this element in states, says,

The modern state, not only in Russia and Germany, but throughout the world, claims to dominate and control the whole life of society and of the individual. Consequently the old conceptions of the relation between Church and State are no longer relevant . . . we are forced to reconsider the whole problem from this new standpoint.[15]

In the same book he becomes still more specific and states,

It may . . . be argued that Communism in Russia, National Socialism in Germany, and Capitalism and Liberal Democracy in the Western countries are fully three forms of the same thing, and that they are all moving by different but parallel paths to the same goal, which is the mechanization of human life and the complete subordination of the individual to the state and to the economic process . . . they are [not] all absolutely equivalent, and we have . . . (a) right to prefer one to another.[16]

Of all the larger states at war during World War II, one of the least totalitarian, it no doubt can be maintained, was the United States. But in dealing with this factor in modern states, Paul Hutchinson finds grounds for a serious charge against the United States government:

How many Americans realize . . . that in the United States there has lately been established a complete rule of the state in the realm of conscience, so that it is now the law of the land, as duly interpreted and affirmed by our highest tribunal, that the good citizen must accept the voice of government as the voice of God? Yet that is the case, the verdict of the Supreme Court to that effect having been rendered in 1931 and never reversed. I have in mind . . . the principle established in the celebrated Macintosh case.[17]

He further charges that the verdict in the case means that now "conscience must accept the dictate of the state!"[18]

It can also be correctly argued, from the human standpoint, that a modern war-making state must necessarily go totalitarian.[19] With these insights it is easy to see that the problem of the Christian and state is upon us with a new intensity. These observations further show that the problem of war for the Christian becomes a central issue in his relations to the state. It is now necessary to bring the total problem into a clearer focus.

Questions for the Believer

The subject of this book—the Christian's relation to the state as taught in the New Testament—has many facets. Perhaps the basic question is that of sovereignty.[20] That God is sovereign, no Bible-believer doubts. The question for the Christian now arises: Is the state sovereign? If so, in what sense? The state exercises a vast amount of authority. By what right does this authority of the state exist? Are there limitations to this authority? When there is conflict between God's authority and that of the State, what must the Christian do? From where does the state derive its authority? This leads to the question of the nature, function, and origin of the state. What does the New Testament say on this vital subject?

The Bible believing Christian must understand from the very nature of his union with Christ and the demands of Scripture that he can exercise only one supreme loyalty. Does not history show that the state has a tendency to invade the area of the Christian's loyalty to God? If loyalty to the state violates his loyalty to God, what must the Christian do?

Perhaps the most central problem in this discussion is the problem of ethics, that is, what action is appropriate for the individual Christian. That the problem is of an ethical character cannot be denied.[21] But is it insoluble?[22] And how is it an ethical problem? Can the state act unethically?[23] Is war and violence unethical if done by the state?[24] Must a state exercise coercion at all?[25] Is there an ethical problem in coercion?[26] Is there an ethical problem in politics for the Christian?[27] Does the Christian have political obligations, or what obligations does the Christian have to the state?

Can the state operate on the principles of New Testament ethics? Can it be governed "in accordance with the law of love"?[28] If the state cannot follow the principles and precepts of New Testament teaching, can the Christian still be involved in the political affairs of government and also give complete obedience to the state?[29] Or must the Christian recognize the possibility that participation in the affairs of state is unethical and that there are times when non-co-operation and disobedience are necessary?[30] If involvement in the state is an ethical problem, is there a dualistic approach to the problem which admits of a double standard of morality, official and private?[31] Or, is personal involvement of such nature that personal guilt is incurred in participation or does the state carry the guilt when such guilt is involved?[32] Such are the ethical questions which must form the core of the problem. This book attempts to discover how the New Testament answers these questions.

Basic Assumptions

The inspiration of Scriptures.—It is impossible to deal with the subject of this book without admitting numerous assumptions. The more fundamental ones will be stated.

The theory of inspiration assumed in dealing with the Bible vitally affects the outcome of any exegesis. It is, therefore, necessary to assume the theory most in accord with Biblical claims. In endeavoring to do this, Gaussen's definition is accepted. He defines inspiration as

> . . . that inexplicable power which the Divine Spirit put forth of old on the authors of holy Scripture, in order to their guidance even in the employment of the words they used, and to preserve them alike from all error and from all omission.[33]

The laws of exegesis. —The laws of exegesis assumed are those which constitute the "Grammatico-Historical" method. This is the "method which most fully commends itself to the judgment and conscience of Christian scholars."[34] The principle in this method is to determine the precise meaning intended by the author. "It applies to the sacred books the same principles, the same grammatical process and exercise of common sense and reason, which we apply to other books."[35]

The unity of the New Testament.—It follows from the above assumption of the definition of inspiration that the New Testament is a unity. A Lundensian scholar speaks of this unity and says, "In spite of all varieties, the New Testament stands out as an extraordinarily firm unity with Christos-Kyrios as its center."[36] This means that no one book or author can be separately interpreted. It also means that no one book or author is obliged to spell out all relevant teaching on a subject, which God has intended to reveal through New Testament writers. With these assumptions accepted, there is no room for contradiction. Rather, all that the New Testament teaches on the subject must be woven into one doctrine and harmonized.

The Old Testament and the problem.—In this book the writer assumes that the Old Testament does not aid materially in the solution of the problem of the Christian's relation to the state. He also assumes that to use the dealings of God with Israel to arrive at conclusions with reference to the problem is not a legitimate use of the Old Testament Scriptures. The basic core of the doctrine must be formulated from the New Testament revelation and the Old Testament can then be used

15

as supplemental material, if the differences of the covenants are clearly borne in mind. A few statements will show the validity of this assumption.

First, God's revelation as embodied in the Bible is progressive.[37] This means that the fuller revelation came last. This revelation has culminated and reached completion in Jesus Christ.[38] Indeed, the writer to the Hebrews calls it a "better" covenant which Jesus established.[39] This "better" element in the covenant is testified to by Christ when he superseded Old Testament revelation with ". . . but I say unto you . . ."[40] Of the necessity of recognizing the principle of progress in revelation, Charles Bigg wrote, ". . . it was this . . . inability to grasp the idea of progress which led to the wholesale importation of ideas and practices from the Old Testament into the Christian Church."[41] It seems clear, therefore that the Old Testament must give way wherever a New Testament principle comes into conflict with Old Testament revelation.

Another support for the assumption is the basic difference between Israel and the Church. The difference is too obvious to need much comment. God dealt with Israel as a religio-civil state. Israel was an earthly nation, even though Israel was more than a nation. The Church, on the other hand, is the mystical body of Christ with a fully spiritual and heavenly calling. Israel as a state was given a body of civil law to enforce.[42] The Church was given the law of love. It is an absolute law. The New Testament enjoins no civil laws for the Christian, neither is the Church called upon to form an autonomous state. It is assumed that the Church will subsist under the secular state.[43]

To Israel, God gave laws which are either directly revoked or at least not permitted as practices of Christians in the New Testament.[44] The ceremonial law is another case in point. This, too, applying to Israel, has been revoked by God for the New Testament Church.[45]

16

Rutenber writes of these aspects of Israel and its status, thus: "The theocratic community, perfectly expressed in the nature of its public order, makes the covenanted people of Jehovah a phenomenon unique in history."[46]

A further significant comment is made by Brunner:

The moral and religious law is blended in one indissoluble unity with the liturgical law of priest, temple and purification on the one hand, and with the law of the state on the other. Hence the law of justice underlying social and political institutions can never be separated from the liturgical laws. If we wish to take over from the Old Testament standards of social and political order, we must take over with them the standards and institution of the cultus, hence the whole apparatus of priest and temple and the laws of governing them.[47]

This does not mean a repudiation of the authority of the Old Testament. Neither is this differentiation the result of a low view of inspiration. It is, rather, the correct distinction between the Old and New Testaments which a sound view of their relationships demands. This view also does no violence to the unity of the Bible. It merely suggests proper usage for the writings of each Covenant. It is, therefore, correct to make the further assumption that where Old Testament revelation will clarify some facet of truth under consideration, it is permissible to make full use of such material.

Four Different Approaches

The writer recognizes that Christian conscience has produced four different "solutions" to the problem of a Christian's relation to the state for Bible-believing Christians. There is first the distinction which is drawn between acting as an individual and privately and as a representative and officially on behalf of society. As an individual the Christian is fully responsible for his moral actions. But when he acts on behalf of the state he is no longer personally responsible for those acts. The state now bears the guilt of those actions. According to Troeltsch, this is essentially the position of Luther.[48] Scott-Craig asserts that the "evangelicals," in essence, have taken up this position.[49] For the Christian this means full participation in politics whatever the nature of the state and absolute obedience to the state is also possible.

Calvin's view is based primarily on the Old Testament. He does not distinguish politics as official action from private actions on the basis of ethics, although he makes a difference between the two by saying, for example, that "the magistrate does not act at all from himself, but merely executes the judgments of God . . ."[50] There is, therefore, to him, no pollution in politics in all of its activities, including "necessary" bloodshed.[51] But the Christian is obligated to take full political responsibility.[52] This he bases on the concept that man stands under a double government, spiritual and political.[53] He thus makes the laws and demands of secular government equivalent to the laws and demands of God, in an absolute sense. He registers at least one mitigating note when he regards the law as condemning all imperfections. Therefore God deals with man "with paternal gentleness." No doubt, Calvin here has reference to the grace of God.

Another view taken by Neo-orthodoxy, accepts personal involvement in the guilt of the state and political action. This creates a moral dualism, but this must simply be accepted.[54] The Christian is freed from this guilt by the grace of God, and is thus free to act in history.[55]

The fourth view does not admit of an ethical dualism either as acting under the forgiving grace of God or as acting in private and official capacities. It considers each act in the light of personal moral responsibility and takes the Gospels and the Epistles seriously in accepting their uncompromising ethical standard for personal action. This is the nonresistant position.

It is evident from this discussion that the differences of the nonresistant position and the other three positions will result in a basic difference in the approach to the problem of the Christian and the state and their relations. Each view will determine largely what those relations will be. The problem involved in these views is a correlative to the larger problem of this book, and must therefore be borne in mind clearly.

Definitions

State and government.—"State" in this discussion means a sovereign, a political and social body, occupying a definite territory, which expresses itself in the government of its people by one of a number of types of human government. Its function is to maintain law and order. To do this it must write its laws and provide means for their enforcement. The protection of its citizens consists in both from invasion from without and molestation from within.[56]

Church.—The term "Church" can be used in more than one way. Basically, the Church is the mystical body of the Lord Jesus Christ[57] which consists of all the regenerate through faith in Him.[58] However, it can also be used in the sense of denominations and local bodies of believers. Each particular usage is to be determined by the context and from the passage itself. At times it is used synonymously with Christendom. In its basic usage the Church is equivalent to the concept of Christians collectively.

Christian.—By this term is meant the individual who has been regenerated by faith in Jesus Christ and is thus transformed and the possession of Christ. The Christian is indwelt by the Spirit of God and is bound by the will of God in his life.

Pacifism.—This discussion uses this term and its other forms to designate the attitude and practice of being opposed to war. It "covers many types of opposition to war. Some modern pacifists are opposed to all wars, and some are not."[59] The motives for their opposition to war are numerous and varied. "Pacifism" as here used, therefore, is a broad term and not to be confused with nonresistance.

Nonresistance.—This term is used to designate that form of belief and practice which abstains from the use of force and violence in the attainment of ends. This principle is applied to private, social, and governmental relations of the Christian. It is applied, also, irrespective of the quality of the ends involved. In its positive aspect, it is the application of the law of love of the New Testament. To those holding this view, it is a question of ethics; but more basically, it is to them a question of absolute obedience to the will of God. Legitimate persuasion and withdrawal are not considered forms of coercion or force.

FOOTNOTES

[1]Ray H. Abrahams, *Preachers Present Arms* (New York: Round Table Press, Inc., 1933), p. 136.

[2]*Ibid.*

[3]*Ibid.*, p. 137.

[4]*Ibid.*

[5]*Ibid.*, p. 217.

[6]Adolf Harnack, *Militia Christi* (Tuebingen: Verlag von J. C. B. Mohr [Paul Siebeck], 1905), p. 55.

[7]Guy Franklin Hershberger, *War, Peace and Nonresistance* (Scottdale: The Herald Press, 1944), p. 298.

[8]Melvin Gingerich, *Service for Peace* (Akron: The Mennonite Central Committee, 1949), pp. 90, 91.

[9]*Ibid.*

[10]Carl F. H. Henry, *The Protestant Dilemma* (Grand Rapids: Wm. B. Eerdmans Publishing Company, 1949), p. 22.

[11]Paul Hutchinson, *The New Leviathan* (Chicago: Willett, Clark, and Company, 1948), pp. 38, 40.

[12]Henry Smith Leiper, *Christ's Way and the World's* (New York: The Abingdon Press, 1936, p. 62.

[13]Emil Brunner, *The Divine Imperative*, trans. Olive Wyon (Philadelphia: The Westminster Press, 1947), pp. 469 ff.

[14]Henry, *op. cit.*, pp. 18-22.

[15]Christopher Dawson, *Religion and the Modern State* (New York: Sheed and Ward, 1940), p. xxii.

[16]*Ibid.*, p. xv.

[17]Hutchinson, *op. cit.*, p. 28.

[18]*Ibid.*, p. 29.

[19]*Ibid.*, p. 37.

[20]Frank Gavin, *Seven Centuries of the Problem of Church and State* (Princeton: Princeton University Press, 1938), p. 4.

[21]Cf. Brunner, *op. cit.*, p. 463.

[22]*Ibid.*

[23]Cf. Nils Ehrenstroem, *Christian Faith and the Modern State,* Denzil Patrick and Olive Wyon (Chicago: Willett, Clark & Company, 1937), p. 124.

[24]Cf. Brunner, *op. cit.,* p. 469.

[25]Rom. 13:4. Cf. Reinhold Niebuhr, *Moral Man and Immoral Society* (New York: Charles Scribner's Sons, 1941), pp. 3, 20, 110.

[26]Cf. Ehrenstroem, *op cit.,* p. 120; Reinhold Niebuhr, *Christian Realism and Political Problems* (New York: Charles Scribner's Sons, 1953), p. 126. A quotation from Augustine.

[27]Niebuhr, *op. cit.,* p. 4; cf. Ehrenstroem, *op. cit.,* p. 115.

[28]Cf. John Christian Wenger, *Separated unto God* (Scottdale: Mennonite Publishing House, 1951), p. 250; cf. Brunner, *op. cit.,* p. 462; cf. Hutchinson, *op. cit.,* p. 168.

[29]Cf. Kenneth G. Grubb (ed.), *The Church and the State* (The Madras Series, VI [New York: International Missionary Council, 1939]), p. 259; cf. Ehrenstroem, *op. cit.,* p. 29; cf. Hutchinson, *op. cit.,* pp. 59, 60.

[30]Cf. Niebuhr, *op. cit.,* p. 257; cf. Brunner, *op. cit.,* p. 481.

[31]Cf. Niebuhr, *op. cit.,* pp. 257, 270 f.; cf. Ernst Troeltsch, *The Social Teaching of the Christian Churches,* trans. Olive Wyon (New York: The Macmillan Company, 1931), II, 507 f.

[32]Cf. Hutchinson, *op. cit.,* pp. 99 f.

[33]L. Gaussen, *Theopneustia* (New and rev. ed.; Cincinnati: George S. Blanchard & Co., 1867), p. 34.

[34]Milton S. Terry, *Biblical Hermeneutics* (Rev. ed.; New York: The Methodist Book Concern, 1911), p. 70.

[35]*Ibid.*

[36]Gustav Aulén, *Church, Law and Society* (New York: Charles Scribner's Sons, 1948), p. 15.

[37]Benjamin B. Warfield, "Revelation," *The International Standard Bible Encyclopedia,* ed. James Orr (5 vols.; Grand Rapids: Wm. B. Eerdmans Publishing Co., 1949), Vol. IV.

[38]Heb. 1:1.

[39]Heb. 8:6.

[40]Matt. 5:28, 32, 34, et cetera.

[41]Charles Bigg, *The Church's Task under the Roman Empire* (Oxford: Clarendon Press, 1905), p. 27.

[42]Hershberger, *op. cit.,* p. 15.

[43]Rom. 13:1-7; cf. Matt. 7:13, 14; Luke 21:10, 11; Dan. 9:26.

[44]Matt. 19:3-9; Exod. 22:18; Lev. 25:44 ff.; Deut. 21:18-21; I Sam. 15.

[45]Heb. 8:13; 10:1; Col. 2:16, 17.

[46]Culbert G. Rutenber, *The Dagger and the Cross* (New York: Fellowship Publications, 1950), p. 69.

[47]Emil Brunner, *Justice and the Social Order*, trans. Mary Hottinger (1st ed.; New York: Harper & Brothers, 1945) pp. 119 f.

[48]Troeltsch, *op. cit.*, II, 489.

[49]T. S. K. Scott-Craig, *Christian Attitudes to War and Peace* (New York: Charles Scribner's Sons, 1938), p. 141.

[50]John T. McNeill (ed.), *John Calvin on God and Political Duty* (New York: The Liberal Arts Press, 1950), pp. 54 f.

[51]*Ibid.*, p. 43.

[52]*Ibid.*, p. xi.

[53]*Ibid.*, pp. xi f.

[54]Niebuhr, *op. cit.*, pp. 270 f.

[55]Niebuhr, *Christianity and Power Politics* (New York: Charles Scribner's Sons, 1940), p. 30.

[56]Wenger, *op. cit.*, p. 245; cf. Anson Phelps Stokes, *Church and State in the United States* (New York: Harper & Brothers, 1950), I, XI.

[57]Eph. 1:22, 23; I Cor. 12.

[58]Heb. 12:23.

[59]Hershberger, *op. cit.*, p. 203.

CHAPTER II

CHURCH HISTORY AND THE CHRISTIAN'S RELATION TO THE STATE

Because the church has always had the problem of its relation to the state on its hands, it is to be expected that church history will make its contribution to the discussion of the problem. It is assumed that the church of the first centuries, because of its spiritual, sociological, and chronological proximity to apostolic Christianity, will have made judgments which must be considered important. The history of the church following the first centuries and its contribution to Christian thinking on this subject helps immeasurably in understanding and focusing the problem.

The Ante-Nicene Period

A brief evaluation of the sources.—The question of the Christian's relation to the state in the church of the first centuries often has been controversial. Especially is this true in the question of its view on the state and war. It is, therefore, necessary to evaluate carefully the sources which have been used in the discussion of this period of church history.

The two most basic and valuable sources are the writings of C. J. Cadoux, a confessed pacifist,[1] and Adolf Harnack, "The German defender of war."[2] Hershberger states that Cadoux is the best authority in the field and brings out that Harnack in his *Militia Christi* does not show the "opposition of the early church to war as sharply as Cadoux does."[3] "Harnack's research did not go as far [he continues] as that of Cadoux, however, and Harnack himself in 1921 cited Cadoux's work (*The Early Christian Attitude to War*) as 'the authoritative conclusion of the investigations made on this question.' "[4]

Another book of significance, covering the same ground, is *The Fall of Christianity*, by G. J. Heering. In writing his review of this book, Bainton makes the following statement of evaluation of the former two writers: "I have recently re-read the sources of this period and am convinced that the picture drawn by Harnack and Cadoux stands the test of scrutiny."[5]

The Social Teaching of the Christian Churches (in two volumes), by Ernst Troeltsch, "is an excellent work . . ."[6] Lastly, Umphrey Lee, *The Historic Church and Modern Pacifism*, must also be mentioned. On the early period of church history he leaned on Harnack.[7]

Until 170 *A.D.*—The first consideration of the problem in the early church until 170 A.D. is that of military service. The church's stand on the "Soldatenfrage" (soldier question) of this period must be gathered from inference.[8] From the fact of silence of the older Christian writings, Harnack infers that there existed no "Soldatenfrage" in the church up to this time.[9] This, he suggests, was for two reasons. One was that the "baptized Christian simply did not become a soldier"[10] (translated from German). The other was that those who became Christians after having enlisted, stayed in the military vocation.[11] However, Cadoux challenges Harnack on this point. He says, as he draws his conclusions of his study on this subject: "With one or two possible exceptions, no soldier joined the Church and remained a soldier until the time of Marcus Aurelius [161-180 A.D.]. Even then, refusal to serve was known to be the normal policy of the Christian . . ."[12]

This latter conclusion seems much more obviously correct because of the view which the early Christians took of war and military service in general. Cadoux, after having quoted profusely from early Christian writers says, "This collection

24

of passages will suffice to show how strong and deep was the early Christian revulsion from and disapproval of war, both on account of the dissension it represented and the infliction of bloodshed and suffering which it involved."[13] Further, "warfare and murder" were closely connected in Christian thought by "their possession of a common element—homicide."[14]

To get a more complete picture of the reasons for the early Christian's abstention from military service, Harnack lists eight factors; only five need to be repeated:

(1) . . . Christianity condemned, on principle, war and bloodshed,

(2) Officers were obliged, under certain conditions, to pass the death sentence and the common soldiers had to carry out whatever they were commanded,

(3) The unconditional military oath . . .,

(4) The Caesar cultus was strongest in the army . . .,

(5) The officers had to sacrifice and the common soldiers had to participate . . .[15] (translated from German.)

From the standpoint of the army, it was possible, as Cadoux sees it, for some Christians to enlist, but there is no evidence that pressure was applied to recruit them.[16] This factor must be borne in mind.

On other aspects of the Christian's relation to the state in this period the early writings are explicit, according to Troeltsch, and can be summed up as follows:

The Early Church . . . retained [the concept] . . . that the . . . "world" is the result of the Fall . . . and a Satanic delusion. The State also sprang from this source, and thus it comes under the uniform and essentially unchangeable principle of the "world," together with all the institutions of marriage, labour, property, slavery, law, and war . . .[17]

In another place he elaborates still further when he says,

Thus Christians took part in all the general conditions of life and industry . . . All offices and callings were barred which had any connection with idol-worship, or with the worship of the Emperor, or those which had anything to do with bloodshed or with capital punishment, or . . . pagan immorality . . . Christians were debarred from taking service under the state or the municipality; they could not serve as judges or as officers in the army; any kind of military service . . . was impossible . . .[18]

25

Cadoux concurs with this conclusion and shows that little is heard of official engagement of Christians in official service in this period.[19]

From 170 A.D. to Constantine.— From 170 A.D. and on, historians are in possession of much material which deals with the question of military service of this period.[20] Cadoux states that now Christians in some numbers were in the army.[21] There are records of the beginning of this period where many soldiers left the army after conversion and some Christians joined who were already converted.[22]

However, it is noteworthy that the church Fathers—Tertullian, Hippolytus, Origen, Cyprian, and Lactantius—as Cadoux shows, objected to military service.[23] Celsus, the pagan philosopher, in his charges against the early Christians, demonstrates this in his writing against Christians.[24] To this must be added the significant statement of Bainton, when he says, "in the period between 100 and 300 A.D., no Christian author whose work is extant condoned Christian participation in warfare."[25]

If these conclusions are accepted, there is here a clear discrepancy between the teaching of the church and the practices of some professing Christians. Bainton, perhaps, has the best interpretation of this phenomenon. He says,

The cleavage might . . . be described as lying between the select and the general mass of Christians. The early church, under the stress of persecution, tended to split on the one hand into smaller bands of ardent spirits, from whom were recruited the martyrs, the bishops, and the writers, and on the other into the rank and file . . . prone to lapse, in persecution to fraternize with the world and to engage in war.[26]

Direct participation of Christians in other affairs of state seem to have taken on similar characteristics. "From the third century onwards . . . Christians became more numerous in the higher ranks of Society and in more eminent professions, in the army, and in official circles."[27]

Schaff, the well-known historian has this to say:

. . . at the time of Diocletian the number of Christians at the court

26

and in the civil office was very considerable . . . [However, generally they] were averse to high office in a heathen state . . . The comparative indifference and particular aversion of the Christians to the affairs of the state, to civil legislation and administration exposed them to the frequent reproach and contempt of the heathens.[28]

Cadoux's conclusions are similar concerning Christians in court and civil office, and he makes the point that "one result of this was to evoke *statements and arguments to the effect that a Christian ought not to hold public office.*"[29]

Litigation was another practice from which the Christians, at least to 250 A.D., seemed to have abstained. No cases are on record according to Cadoux where a Christian impleads a wrongdoer before a pagan court, although sitting in judgment on civil suits, Tertullian seemingly regarded as harmless.[30]

Rulers were considered appointed of God. In this, evidently, no difference was made between good and wicked rulers.[31] Generally, the church held to submission to the magistrates, but the Christians reserved to themselves the "right of . . . disobeying the laws and orders of the state, whenever those . . . came into conflict with . . . the law of God."[32] The Pauline injunction of prayer for government officials seems to have been followed by Christians.[33]

The Post-Nicene Period

The sudden change.—In the beginning of the fourth century momentous changes occurred in both state and church. The Edict of Milan, essentially an edict of freedom for Christianity,[34] paved the way for allying church and state.[35] To become a "Christian" soon became the only religiously honorable thing to do.[36] Paganism was soon to condition Christianity in an unprecedented way because of its influx into the church.[37] It must be admitted that there were factors in the church previous to Constantine which anticipated some decline of the church;[38] but the decline now was sudden.

The theologians now employed their pens to analyze war. They declared in favor of the necessity of just wars and a Christian participation in them. Athanasius, Ambrose, and

27

Augustine were the *first* Christian theologians to try to "harmonize war and the Gospel."[39] *Prima facie,* this seems strong evidence that the church up to this point had not regarded war as just. The change of view on war came to a climax when in 416 A.D. "non-Christians were forbidden to serve in the army."[40]

The church was now an auxiliary to civil government.[41] Full mutual participation was now the order of the day. The separation of church and state was past history. But full participation in the affairs of the "world" was not the only way the new situation was met by Christians. Monasticism and the sectarian churches were two other alternatives.

The development.—The new synthesis of church and state, having brought about drastic changes in the church and its relationship to the state, was not long in spawning a new idea. Ambrose and Augustine, evidently, were the first to give voice to it. It is most likely that they did not perceive the full impact the new concept might have. The logic of Ambrose seems clear. He argued, according to Sabine, that in spiritual matters the church has the jurisdiction over all Christians, the emperor included, for he is in the church. Thus he stated boldly, ". . . bishops are wont to judge of Christian emperor, not emperor of bishops" (quoted by Sabine).[42]

Augustine, although not consciously teaching the rulership of church over state, actually, says Neve, "offered a foundation that was used by the hierarchy after his time" as a basis for the concept of primacy of the church in civil affairs.[43] This idea in Augustine came from his development of the concept of *de civitate Dei.* This *civitas* was a city or organized community, but it actually was represented by the visible organized church.[44] By the time of Gregory the Great, through political and religious circumstances, the church was a civil power.

The Medieval Period

The Catholic concept.—From Gregory on, the theory of the "church-state" developed. The church was equivalent to the

Corpus Christianum. This meant that society as a state and society as the church were co-extensive. But the state was an instrument in the hands of the church. This theocratic concept of government—God ruling through the church—came to its height under popes like Gregory VII[45] to Boniface VIII.[46]

After this, while the concept remained, the church lost the power to approximate that concept in practice.

It is interesting to note, as Bainton develops it, that under this theocracy a new concept of war developed. Pacifism was associated with the concept of the separation of church and state. The just-war theory was a corollary of the union of church and state, and "the crusading idea" the corollary of a theocracy.[47] Under pacifism the church rejects war. Under the just-war theory war and participation in it is permitted, although participation is commonly reluctant. The crusade is holy. Under his theory it is the church which wages war, "and without qualms."[48] The phrase *"Ecclesia abhorret a sanguine"* is no longer true in this concept.[49]

A word must be said of Thomas Aquinas and his view of the state. He laid the foundation for subsequent Catholic thought on the subject. Ehrenstroem finds Thomas' teaching that the state is of the order of nature.[50] It therefore is the natural foundation for the church.[51] In view of these facts it "exists in the Providence of God,"[52] but the church was, as Heering understands Thomas, the order of grace which was the highest order.[53] Thus the Catholic theocracy was a philosophic principle.

In spite of all this synthetizing, the Roman Church was still obliged to acknowledge a dual standard because there were keen consciences which felt the tension between earthly and heavenly citizenship. The accepted cloister life was one such acknowledgment.[54]

Dissenting views.—The dissenting views against medieval Catholic thought on church and state are generally from two sources. One source was political. It came from within the

Roman fold. It clamored for a type of separation between the two. Marsilio of Padua went farthest of the medieval writers in "setting apart the spiritual and religious from the legal," says Sabine.[55] But even he did not know of separation of church and state as the term is commonly understood today.

The other voice came from the sectarian groups. Their cry was to go back to primitive Christianity.[56] Their motives were usually spiritual and religious and not political. Many of these people were pacifists. They abhorred bloodshed, and in general were "withdrawal" sects.[57] As far as we know, the Waldenses took no part in government.[58]

The Reformation Period

Luther.—Luther's theology contained inconsistencies. His view on the Christian's relation to the state was no exception. Of this Sabine has to say that, "His political opinions were too much governed by circumstances."[59]

On the one side Luther taught, as Troeltsch shows,

Over and over again, in countless passages, the characteristic principles of this ethic, which consists in aloofness from the world, and in the concentration of attention upon the question of personal salvation and of the unity of the brethren in the love of God. He also makes it quite plain that this ethic of love and salvation is opposed to the ethic which is produced by the struggle for existence, with its concern with questions relating to law, honour, war, the State, and retribution. The Christian is actually only concerned with the life of the world on the side of his physical existence, because his life is temporarily involved in the conditions of earthly existence. To him the real laws of Christian behaviour are those laid down by the Sermon on the Mount . . ."[60]

These concepts are primarily found in his earlier writings.[61] His pragmatic considerations later dictated a different course of thought. He soon succumbed to the concept of complete passive obedience. At this point he became wholly in accord with Calvin.[62] But here came the clash. This was an ethical problem. He finds his solution in the famous dualistic ethic. It is because of his dualistic concept that Luther could teach without qualms, seemingly, to do the worst to the rebels in the peasant war.[63]

But his concept of passive obedience caused another inconsistency to arise. In the struggle of the Lutheran cause there were occasions where the prince was in collision with the emperor, on behalf of Luther. Luther's pragmatic decision, as shown by Sabine, was in favor of passive obedience to the prince.[64]

There was, then, a movement in the view of Luther, from a more sectarian viewpoint toward the position of Calvin as far as practice is concerned.

Calvin.—The position of Calvin has been stated in a previous connection.[65] Only a few statements need be added. Calvin was more consistent than Luther. Unconditional submission was obligatory whether rulers were good or bad.[66] If Troeltsch can be followed, it seems that Calvin felt no necessity of harmonizing the gospel ethic with complete participation in the society of the world.[67] His theocratic viewpoint practically equated the law of the state with the law of God.[68]

The Anabaptists.—The Anabaptists, not including the Muensterites and a number of fringe elements, were opposed both to the Christianity of Catholicism and the Reformers. Their ideal was the primitive Christianity of the New Testament.[69] They considered the ethic of the New Testament binding on the Christian in its obvious interpretation and refused to accept any type of dualistic approach which would suggest two kinds of morality.

As a consequence, they believed in full discipleship to Christ of every believer. Discipleship was to them the proof of regeneration. A total life of love and as a necessary corollary—nonresistance—was part of this discipleship. "The world," the contemporary social order outside of the true Christian church, was to be shunned.[70]

The result of these concepts was the theory that no Christian could hold political office. Military service was contrary to the ethic of New Testament and so sinful. The oath could not be taken because of the direct command of Jesus and James.

In other words, there was to be a total separation between the Christians and the state. Yet, in spite of these ideals, they accepted the state as a necessity for a sinful world[71] and passive resistance was only permitted when the demands of state violated the Christian conscience. Otherwise a full submissive and active obedience to the state was enjoined.

The Post-Reformation Period

The four basic attitudes and concepts as have been traced through history to post-Reformation era are virtually the views which have been held by Christendom till the present. However, in their historical development, modifications and elaborations can be noticed.

The Roman Catholic view of the theocracy has not died. Rather, because of political world conditions it is merely submerged, only to partially show its existence from time to time.[72]

The Calvinistic trend, beginning with Calvin's successor, Beza, because of historical expedients, reversed its concept of passive obedience to the state. The Calvinists now, as Sabine points out, urged the right of resistance to "tyranny."[73] This meant that the theocratic concept of Calvin was not totally accepted.

Lutheranism, on the other hand, with its "solution" to the moral problem involved, moved fully to the position of obedience which Calvinism abandoned.

The Anabaptistic view was perpetuated in some of the smaller sects.

The era of nationalism with its correlative of patriotism plus the concept of the divine origin of the state held by large segments of the church[74] had its effect upon Christendom. The effect is especially seen in conjunction with the just-war theory. It was now not some ultimate or dogmatic truth which formed the basis for determining whether a war was just or not. It was rather emotional patriotism which decided the issue. Thus, whatever war the state fought was the "just" war. The book, *Preachers Present Arms*, gives evidence of this.[75]

But Christendom has been somewhat awakened from its slumber. A consciousness of the supra-national character of Christianity has been more evident in recent years in the Christian church. The results of this type of outlook necessarily will condition the church's view of the Christian's relation to the state. A new analysis and evaluation of the problem, as has been intimated, has already begun. For the Bible-believing Christian, however, no theory of this relation which is not built squarely on the inspired Word of God can be acceptable.

FOOTNOTES

[1]Roland Bainton, "The Christian and War," *The Christian Century,* LXI (May 3, 1944), 560. This is a review of the book, *The Fall of Christianity,* by G. J. Heering.

[2]*Ibid.*

[3]Hershberger, *op. cit.,* p. 72.

[4]*Ibid.*

[5]Bainton, *op. cit.,* p. 560.

[6]Hershberger, *op. cit.,* p. 72.

[7]Cf. *Ibid.*

[8]Harnack, *op. cit.,* p. 47.

[9]*Ibid.*

[10]*Ibid.,* p. 49.

[11]*Ibid.*

[12]C. John Cadoux, *The Early Christian Attitude to War* (London: Headley Bros. Publishers, Ltd., 1919), p. 245.

[13]*Ibid.,* p. 57.

[14]*Ibid.*

[15]Harnack, *op. cit.,* p. 46.

[16]Cecil John Cadoux, *Christian Pacifism Re-examined* (Oxford: Basil Blackwell, 1940), p. 67.

[17]Troeltsch, *op. cit.,* p. 147.

[18]*Ibid.,* p. 123.

[19]Cadoux, *The Early Church and the World, passim.*

[20]Harnack, *op. cit.,* p. 53.

[21]Cadoux, *The Early Christian Attitude to War,* p. 105.

[22]*Ibid.*, p. 245.

[23]*Ibid.*, p. 256.

[24]Cf. Alexander Roberts and James Donaldson (eds.), *The Ante-Nicene Fathers* (Buffalo: The Christian Literature Publishing Company, 1885), IV, 667 f. The basis for this statement is taken from the writing of *Origen against Celsus*, Bk. VIII, chaps. lxxiii-lxxv.

[25]Bainton, *op. cit.*, p. 560.

[26]*Ibid.*

[27]Troeltsch, *op. cit.*, p. 125.

[28]Philip Schaff, *History of the Christian Church* (Grand Rapids: Wm. B. Eerdmans Publishing Company, 1950), II, 345 f.

[29]Cecil John Cadoux, *The Early Church and the World* (Edinburgh: T. & T. Clark, 1925), p. 360.

[30]*Ibid.*, p. 366.

[31]*Ibid.*, p. 379.

[32]*Ibid.*, p. 528.

[33]*Ibid.*, pp. 180, 363.

[34]Cf. Lars P. Qualben, *A History of the Christian Church* (Rev.; New York: Thomas Nelson and Sons, 1951), p. 116, but the main source is, Henry Bettenson (ed.), *Documents of the Christian Church* (Oxford: University Press, 1943), p. 22.

[35]Schaff, *op. cit.*, III, 4, 131.

[36]Albert Henry Newman, *A Manual of Church History* (rev. ed.; Philadelphia: The American Baptist Publication Society, 1947), I, 307, 313.

[37]*Ibid.*, I, 313 f.

[38]Qualben, *op. cit.*, p. 114.

[39]Heering, *op. cit.*, p. 37.

[40]Cadoux, *The Early Christian Attitude to War*, p. 257.

[41]*Ibid.*, p. 258.

[42]George H. Sabine, *A History of Political Theory* (New York: Henry Holt and Company, 1950), p. 187.

[43]J. L. Neve, *A History of Christian Thought* (Philadelphia: The United Lutheran Publication House, 1943), I, 104 f.

[44]Cf. Qualben, *op. cit.*, p. 126.

[45]*Ibid.*, pp. 167 f.

[46]*Ibid.*, p. 181.

[47]Bainton, *op. cit.*, p. 560.

[48]*Ibid.*

[49]Umphrey Lee, *The Historic Church and Modern Pacifism* (New York: Abingdon-Cokesbury Press, 1943), p. 77.

[50]Ehrenstroem, *op. cit.*, p. 24

[51]Heering, *op. cit.*, p. 72.

[52]*Ibid.*

[53]*Ibid.*

[54]*Ibid.,* p. 73.

[55]Sabine, *op. cit.,* p. 299.

[56]E. H. Broadbent, *The Pilgrim Church* (London: Pickering & Inglis, 1931), p. 97.

[57]*Ibid.,* p. 98.

[58]*Ibid.,* p. 100.

[59]Sabine, *op. cit.,* p. 361.

[60]Troeltsch, *op. cit.,* II, 495.

[61]*Ibid.,* p. 496.

[62]Cf. Lee, *op. cit.,* p. 132.

[63]Newman, *op. cit.,* II, 80.

[64]Sabine, *op. cit.,* p. 361.

[65]*Vide supra.,* p. 17

[66]Sabine, *op. cit.,* p. 366.

[67]Troeltsch, *op. cit.,* II, 599.

[68]Cf. Sabine, *op. cit.,* p. 366.

[69]Harold S. Bender, "The Anabaptist Vision", *The Mennonite Quarterly Review.,* XVIII (April, 1944), p. 83.

[70]*Ibid.*

[71]C. Henry Smith, *The Story of the Mennonites* (3d ed.; Newton: Mennonite Publication Office, 1950), p. 23.

[72]Augustine J. Osgniach, *The Christian State* (Milwaukee: The Bruce Publishing Company, 1943), pp. 306 ff.

[73]Sabine, *op. cit.,* p. 377.

[74]Cf. Ehrenstroem, *op. cit.,* p. 97.

[75]Abrams, *op. cit., passim.*

CHAPTER III

JESUS AND THE CHRISTIAN'S RELATION TO THE STATE

Jesus' Teaching

In the Synoptic Gospels.—The first Biblical passage we shall examine is Christ's temptation.[1] This passage does not contain any direct teaching of Christ with reference to the subject under discussion, except by implication. Only the third temptation (in Luke the second)[2] is pertinent to the inquiry. It is the temptation built around Satan's offer to give Christ "the kingdom of the world" (*tas basileias tou kosmou*).[3]

The problem which arises out of the temptation is whether Satan has any relationship to the state, and if so, what it is. To determine this, three questions must be answered. First, was Satan's offer based on fact when he assumed the power to give Christ the kingdoms? Second, what is meant by the term "world"? And third, what is meant by "kingdoms"?

According to the assumptions stated in the introduction, it must be granted that the temptation of Jesus was a *bona fide* temptation. The narrative carries all the evidences of being intended to be history. As such, the facts are reported as they occurred. When Satan tempted Christ, there is no retort by Christ that Satan's statement is not true. With these facts in mind, one is driven to conclude that either Christ was ignorant at this point, and thus, because of this ignorance, this constituted a real temptation to Him; or to the other alternative that Christ was not ignorant at this point but rather, he as the Son of God, with supernatural knowledge,[4] knew that Satan was speaking the truth.

The Lukan account introduces additional elements into the narrative.[5] Here Satan adds that the authority over the kingdoms has been given to him and he disposes of this authority at will.

In view of these considerations it seems that, whatever the "kingdoms of the world" are, they are in some real way under the control of Satan. Weiss and others[6] concur with this conclusion and Weiss adds, "This can be conceived of only in one way, viz., that, in a world which is in the service of sin, he turns men's hearts according to his will."[7]

According to Thayer, the occurrence of "kingdom" in these passages has the meaning of "the territory subject to the rule of a king."[8] With this New Testament exegetes agree. This would then be equivalent to the modern concept of state.

In the place of world (*kosmos*) in Matthew, Luke uses world (*oikoumene*). The former term has a broader meaning than the latter one. But the usage of these terms makes it clear that it is the "whole inhabited earth, the world" which is meant. From the way Thayer defines the Lukan term, the only limitation which could be placed on the meaning of world would be that it did not include the barbarians outside the Roman empire.[9] However in view of these parallel passages this restriction is clearly not intended here.

In conclusion it can be noticed that while the emphasis in *basileia* is rulership, the emphatic element in *oikoumene* is men. And the emphasis of *kosmos* "brings out the orderly arrangement of the universe . . ."[10] Bringing these emphases together makes this passage point to the concept of Satan ruling in the orderly society of men and the state. A final conclusion must not yet be drawn. This intepretation is in profound agreement with the further teaching of Christ and the apostles as will be evident in a later part of this discussion.

The Sermon on the Mount

Perhaps one of the most acute exegetical battlegrounds of the New Testament has been the Sermon on the Mount. One of the greatest problems in this section of the teaching of Christ have been His statements about nonresistance and love. It is not suggested that Christ's Sermon contains express commands which are directly applied to the problem of the Christian and the state. However, the fact that it carries material relevant to the question of nonresistance makes it pertinent to this book.

There is another reason for focusing attention on a part of the Sermon on the Mount. This reason also supplies the clue as to what part of the Sermon[11] should be examined. The reason consists in the fact that Jesus lifts out of the records of the Hebrew civil legislation,[12] as given by God, the principle,[13] upon which all just law and its administration is built.[14] As such, the passage is most relevant to this discussion, because this *jus talionis*[15] (the law of retaliation) was a factor, not only in the Hebrew nation, and in the Roman state, but also is basic in civil and criminal law today.

The reason, that the Lord's teaching of love[16] is also included in this examination, is based on the obvious unity of the whole passage examined. Jesus first made the negative statement of nonresistance. Then he made the positive statement describing why resistance must not be practiced. He also showed what must take the place of resistance. This is love.

Another crucial question which needs examination is to whom the Sermon on the Mount was spoken, and who are meant to practice the moral precepts laid down in it. It does not fall into the scope of this discussion to determine whether the Lukan and Matthean accounts of the Sermon are narratives of the same event. It is the content of teaching which is significant to this examination. It is, however, essential to note that in each case the writers seem to show that Christ addressed the disciples to the exclusion of the multitude.[17] The repetition of the addressing pronoun emphasizes this fact.[18]

An element in the Sermon which clearly indicates restrictive application of its teaching is the type of people Christ recognizes its recipients to be.[19] These can only be those who stand in union with Christ. The fact that Paul uses parts of the Sermon on the Mount for "teaching to control the moral behaviour of the Christian community . . ."[20] is further evidence that its teachings were meant for Christians.[21] No doubt, Paul was correct in this application because Christ had already said that the disciples were to teach the regenerated "to observe all things whatsoever I have commanded you."[22]

An implication which can be deduced from this consideration is that the Sermon on the Mount is not a legal code for a sinful society or the world at large. This seems to be shown by Christ specifically by the way He dealt with the *jus talionis*. Christ did not abrogate the principle. To have done so would have made the institution of human government in a sinful society impossible.[23] But what Christ does is to say that the disciple must not apply this principle in his dealing with his fellow men.

Windisch's conclusion concerning the question for whom these injunctions of Christ are meant seems to be correct. He says, ". . . in the Sermon on the Mount, the typical disciple in the eyes of Jesus is not the poor sinner who cries for redemption, but the servant of God who is wholly obedient to his Lord."[24]

The implications from the foregoing arguments are that the teaching of Christ in the Sermon has immediate and present validity for the Christian. As is evident, therefore, neither the theory, held by some dispensationalists, that the rules of life presented in the Sermon are postponed in their applications,[25] nor the theory that it constitutes an interim ethic,[26] which is impractical for the present age, can be accepted.

However, this does not mean that every statement in it must be applied literally, for to do so would be the height of folly and contradictory even to the Sermon itself.[27] But it means that where figurative language is used, there spiritual and ethical principles must be deduced. It also means that where it can be determined that the language is literal, there Jesus evidently expected a literal fulfillment of the demand.

Christ commences this section[28] of His teaching in the Sermon by using the now familiar statement, "Ye have heard that it hath been said . . ." Then follows the Old Testament quotation: ". . . An eye for an eye, and a tooth for a tooth . . ."[29] The first problem is to determine what Christ meant when He used this quotation. What did He intend that the disciples should understand? Two basic factors must be borne in mind in the interpretation of this statement. One is: What does this statement mean in its Old Testament setting? The other is: How was it used in contemporary Judaism?

As has already been stated, the statement finds its setting in the Old Testament, and—in all three instances—in the civil precepts which the Hebrews were to follow.[30] The expression amounts, in these settings, to a statement of principle based on literal exactions in some areas of civil and criminal justice.

From this it follows that this *jus talionis* is basically meant for the administration of justice. As such it is not permissible to conclude that it was meant in a restrictive sense, (that is to restrict retaliation), primarily, as some would seem to indicate.[31] Rather, it was meant equally in a restrictive sense and the sense of redressing the wronged one for wrong done to him. It was equally meant to restrict the wronged one who had the power to retaliate and in vengeance might succeed in inflicting more on the evil-doer than the justice of equality would permit, as it was meant to recompense the one who was wronged and yet did not have the power to force repayment for his wrong. That the element of redress for wrong is included in this law is freely admitted by Bruce in his exposition of the synoptic gospels.[32] It is also clearly borne out in the context of these passages in the Old Testament. For example, in the Leviticus passage from which the New Testament quotation is taken, the context speaks of the killing of an Israelite's beast as well as shedding human blood. With reference to the case, when one man's beast was killed by another, the killer was obliged to "make it good, life for life."[33] It seems that the conclusion here must be that the redress for wrong was meant as much as the idea of retaliation.

The exaction of payment of a fine to one who has been wounded in a fight, for the lost time of the wounded man,[34] and the payment for a killed ox when under certain circumstances another man's ox has done it,[35] are evidences of the fact that redress was involved as much as a restriction of the inflicting of vengeance.

Another factor which indicates that God intended the *jus talionis* for more than just a restriction of retaliation is the purpose for which He instituted it. The purpose was to curb crime and sin and to maintain civil order among the Hebrews. Moses puts it thus:

. . . so shalt thou put away the evil from the midst of thee. And those that remain shall hear, and fear, and shall henceforth commit no more any such evil in the midst of thee. And thine eyes shall not pity; life *shall go* for life, eye for eye, tooth for tooth, hand for hand, foot for foot.[36]

Further significant weight is lent to this argument when Moses specifically commands that "Thou shalt not take vengeance, nor bear any grudge against the children of thy people," and enjoins love for one another.[37]

The conclusion, then, must be that the injunction was not a permission to exercise private and hateful vengeance in the sense in which the word is often used currently. But it was more basically the punishment of the guilty person, which was based on the law of Moses by procedure of the Israelitish courts.

The New Testament usage of "vengeance" (*ekdikesis*) and "revenger" (*ekdikos*) in Romans twelve and thirteen, respectively, must carry this meaning, as is seen from Romans 13:4. Of the usage of the former word in the New Testament generally, the best Greek lexicographical authority has this to say, ". . . the meaning of *ekdikesis* in the New Testament . . . [is] vengeance, requital, punishment, mostly the last"[38] (translated from German). The fuller meaning, taking the usage and roots of these words into consideration, is to mete out punishment on the basis and with the intent of justice.

However, the Jewish contemporaries of Jesus evidently had more than this in mind when they used the words which Jesus here used. Broadus says that, "The Jews held that this law justified personal retaliation of private wrongs and self-defense."[39]

In view of these conclusions, what did the Lord mean when He said to His disciples, contrasting His new injunction with that of the Old Testament, "resist not him that is evil?" If the conclusions which have been made are admitted, Christ meant that when the disciples have been privately wronged, they must not seek revenge or redress through legal or coercive means. All those doing evil to the Christians are meant, and are explicitly called enemies in the context. If, then, the disciples were not permitted to exercise the rights by coercion or the legal process, it must follow that private retaliation was doubly ruled out. Windisch concurs with these conclusions and says, "If the old law permitted retaliation, self-defense, and prosecution, the new lawgiver forbids all this. No self-defense is permitted. On the contrary, there is to be renunciation of all legal right and plaint."[40]

"Evil" (*to ponero*) has here been construed as "the civil man." It means the one who injures[41] the Christian or seeks his injury. This seems to be the only valid interpretation. It cannot mean the devil, because Peter and other writers call upon the Christian to resist him.[42] Again, the emphasis in this passage is on a person to person relationship. Jesus' meaning cannot include evil in the sense of calamity or injury as such because morality is not involved in these. Viewing the Lord's statement, enjoining love for enemies,[43] as necessarily supplemental to the injunction of nonresistance, makes this interpretation the only valid one.

What Jesus meant, then, in teaching nonresistance is that the Christian was to abstain from all use of force or coercion, whether legal or physical, for the purpose of subduing the "evil man," or for the righting of wrong done by him. This nonresistance does not exclude stern rebuke,[44] petition,[45] nor does it include willful exposure to evil and injury.[46] The relationship of Christ's example to His teaching, which is here assumed, will find discussion later.

However, in these conclusions there exists an implication which clarifies the concept of nonresistance which Jesus had in mind. It has been charged that, if the course of nonresistance is followed, no evil would be resisted[47] and justice would be supplanted by anarchy and *no order would exist.* This charge has often been made,[48] but the charge is unfounded. One reason for the groundlessness of the charge will be considered later in this chapter. One must be stated briefly at this point.

Whatever Christ said when enjoining nonresistance was said in the full view of the facts of future history based on His foreknowledge and the providence of God.[49] Looking back upon history from the present vantage point, it can now be seen what Jesus knew when He made the pronouncement of nonresistance. He knew that relative justice would always be administered. He also knew that in a society where a supreme love does not operate, justice *must* operate. It should therefore be noticed that Jesus does not, in teaching this principle, set aside the *jus talionis* (the law of retaliation).[50] Rather, He is simply telling His disciples that they, as Christians, must not be the ones who apply the *jus talionis.* Neither must they be instrumental in employing it. The implication further suggests that a society which needs the administration of justice will

43

have, relatively speaking, the *jus talionis* to use. It is this application of relative justice based on the *jus talionis* without which, it is evident, order could not exist in sinful society.

Jesus' view finds further substantiation in the Scriptures. His whole teaching of this age and its end shows that he anticipated a sinful society to exist.[51] Further, He clearly assumed that states—human governments—would exist till His coming. This can be gathered both from a specific statement[52] and from the fact that Christ predicted that wars would continue till the end.[53] Wars necessarily imply states under the dominion of sin. And so, it can be said that the Lord already anticipated Paul[54] and Peter[55] in their classical utterances on the function of the state and the Christian's relation to it, or, perhaps, the apostles understood Christ in this way and passed on their teaching as approximating Christ's.[56] Brunner, no doubt, is correct when he makes the observation that "the characteristic element in the Sermon on the Mount is the fact that it expounds the law of love without taking the claims of the 'official order' into consideration at all."[57] But the question which Brunner has not answered is: For what reason did Christ not do so?

After having given the teaching of nonresistance to the disciples, the Lord uses four examples to clarify His pronouncement. In each case the nonresistance teaching is strongly stated, and in each case the Christian is not to depend on justice but rather suffer instead.

These four examples are related to four different types of encounter with the "enemy" who may cause injury to the Christian. The first example[58] is given of the area of personal insult and bodily injury or personal violence.[59] The slight overstatement in this statement, as also in the following two examples, if the interpretation of verse 39a is accepted, is made for the sake of emphasis,[60] especially in the sense of repetition of injury. The second example[61] is from the area of litigation.[62] (*krithenai*) "to sue at law" is the meaning here.[63] The Christian must not resist. The third example[64] is from the area of forced service to government.[65] The fourth example[66] is from the area of personal property. Here, too, resistance to the evil man who would injure, must not be practiced.

The negative injunction—to "resist not him that is evil"— has been considered. But this injunction is based on the positive injunction to love. The final verses of Matthew chapter five enjoin the positive conduct of the Christian to his fellow man which forms the basis for the concept of nonresistance.

Again the Lord starts with the familiar saying: "Ye have heard . . ."[67] He then makes a statement which is partly an Old Testament quotation and partly what evidently was a popular maxim of His day.[68] Again Jesus went beyond the Old Testament injunction in His teaching. The Jewish attitude toward their enemies He positively contradicted. He said, "but I say unto you, Love your enemies, and pray for them that persecute you . . ."[69]

Who is the neighbor (*plesion*[70]) and who is the (*echthros*[71])? The answer to these questions is essential to understanding Christ's command to the Christian to love. Again the Old Testament and the contemporary backgrounds must be considered. The injunction to love one's neighbor, which Jesus quotes, He took from Leviticus 19:18. In this verse there are two parallel nounal designations used synonymously. They are: "The children of thy people" and "neighbor." The previous verse has "brother" and "neighbor" as parallel nouns. An examination of the two verses and their context shows that obviously all of these refer to the same person or persons. These persons are Israelites. The fact, therefore, is that from the standpoint of the Old Testament the neighbor is a member of the Jewish nation.[72]

The contemporary Jewish concept of neighbor was identical to the Old Testament view. The synagogue at the time of Jesus defined "neighbor" ". . . as narrowly as the O.T. . . . [and] those not Israelites do not fall into this concept."[73] (Translated from German.)

However, there is evidently in the context of the New Testament passage the idea of contrast. Neighbor (*plesion*) is contrasted with enemy (*echthros*). This indicates that the concept of neighbor used by Jesus has the idea of friendliness and mutuality. The one who seeks to harm a person is the enemy. This observation must follow in view of the preceding verses.

The enemy (*echthros*) was to the Jewish mind the Gentile.[74] It was to them, therefore, an all inclusive term. It was construed in terms of a national enemy, a private enemy, and also a religious enemy.[75] But Christ's usage is that whoever injures, or violates another person is an enemy to the one who is thus violated. Now the command of Christ is to love that person. Jesus takes for granted that the neighbor will be loved. But His injunction is to love the enemy. What does Christ mean with this command? What does this love (*agapao*) mean?

Agapao "denotes the highest, most perfect kind of love . . . implying a clear determination of will and judgment . . ."[76] It, therefore, does not depend upon the nature or "lovableness" of the object of love. As is clear from Paul's usage, love (*agape*) will not do any ill to any man.[77] To the contrary, love can only do good.[78] This is the kind of love with which God loves. This is clear from the fact that Jesus uses the example of God's love in His impartial dealing with the world of saints and sinners as demonstrating what the Christian's love must be. As such, love must not only not do ill or harm but must go beyond that and do positive good to the very ones who seek the Christian's hurt. This includes praying for enemies. This is clearly the positive aspect of the conduct of a Christian on which the negative aspect of nonresistance is based.

Quell and Stauffer give a good summary of Christ's meaning of love in this passage; they write:

The love of enemies, demanded by Jesus, characterizes the attitude of the sons of the new people of God, to whom the future belongs, towards the children of this world. They must practice love without expecting any return, lend where there is not hope of repayment, give away with boundless generosity. They must willingly accept the world's hostility in a sacrificial spirit of nonresistance . . . even doing good to those who hate them, countering curses with blessing and praying for their persecutors . . . This unparalleled will to martyrdom goes far . . . A new task of intercession is here laid upon the martyr: he is to pray for the hostile world, which hates God and kills the faithful. [79]

The final statement[80] which Jesus makes in this section of the Sermon on the Mount is the summary statement as to how the Christian must love. It is still the Christian's love for his enemies. It is to be a perfect love like God's love is perfect. Nothing is said about the possibility or impossibility of such loving for the child of God. But his love is not complete until he loves as God loves. To say, "I cannot love thus, therefore I am permitted to love less," is antinomianistic. In other words, the fact that the Christian cannot attain the absolute ideal gives him no permission to do less than the ideal.[81] If this conclusion is warranted, it applies to the whole teaching of love and nonresistance as here taught by Jesus.

A further examination of this love of God as is presented to the Christian as supreme example to follow must be made. It is clear from Jesus' statement of the nature of God's love, that, from the positive standpoint it is the impartation of bountiful good to the objects of His love—"on the just and the unjust." But there is here presented a negative aspect of God's love which is as important to the context of this passage of the Sermon on the Mount as the positive. The positive aspect is connected with Christ's teaching concerning the actual love for enemies. The negative aspect is related to the teaching of nonresistance more precisely, although, as has already been shown, these different aspects make up the indivisible moral conduct of love.

This negative aspect of God's love is His suspension of direct justice in the dealing with His "enemies" which are, of course, the world. In that God loves the unjust, according to this passage, He has suspended the direct administration of justice with reference to them. If God dealt with the unjust according to His justice they could not be the partakers of the common grace. Again, it must be emphasized, this does not mean that Jesus meant that there would be no justice operative in the world; it means that the justice which operates on the human level is not the immediate justice of God. It means that there are other factors and agencies which produce the relatively just order in a sinful society. Neither does it mean that God condones the injustices of men or does not desire them to do justly. It means that He does not *now* enforce justice among them.[82] This is the example in nonresistance which the Christian must follow.

One word must be said about the relation of love to justice. As love has been defined, it is always more than justice.[83] And being more, it always fulfills justice.[84] The Christian, then, as a doer of the law of love, is also a doer of justice. It follows, therefore, that love actually embodies justice. The practicing of love, then, is not an annulling of justice; it is the fulfillment of it. This means that when Jesus gave the injunction to love, He actually put His approval upon justice. To repeat, however, He showed that it did not fall within the area of Christian obligation or privilege to administer or demand justice.

Some Conclusions

In concluding this study of a section of the Sermon on the Mount, a few summary observations must be made. It has been concluded that Jesus taught a concept of nonresistance. That this nonresistance is bound up in the whole concept of love as commanded by Jesus is plain. Although Christ's usage of "enemies" and His reference to "persecution" point toward a broader application of the teaching of Christ than merely to private or personal relation, yet this will not now be pressed at this point. And, what has been clear is that Jesus was making a full application of the laws of love and nonresistance to the individual Christian. However, even this restricted application immediately gives occasion for posing a number of most crucial problems. First, did Christ imply that what a Christian could not do on his own behalf he could still, without penalty, do on behalf of another? Second, may the Christian do as a representative of society, e.g., the state, what God has forbidden him to do for himself personally? [85] Or, must the Christian take the attitude that, in spite of the commandment of Jesus, since he cannot attain the ideal, he must, therefore, participate in the sins of a sinful society, and depend upon the grace of God?[86] Or, third, must the Christian take the command of nonresistance seriously and take the position that he can never act in any other capacity but a personal capacity and therefore whenever an act incurs guilt he must abstain completely, irrespective of the most severe consequence to his person? Has Christ answered these questions, or has He left them unanswered? The answer which one gives to these crucial questions will largely constitute the basis for a view of the Christian's relation to the state.

As indicated by the footnotes, serious Christians have given affirmative answer to all the above questions. Windisch writes of the third concept and the Christians who hold this view as it relates to the Sermon on the Mount. He says,

. . . they cannot simply be dismissed as "fanatics" or "sectarian." If this is what they are, then Jesus himself was a fanatic and the founder of a sect. The unmistakable conclusion of our exegesis is that such people have correctly understood the Sermon on the Mount. The Sermon intends to proclaim commands. It presents demands that are to be literally understood and literally fulfilled. Polemic against "fanatics" is to a large extent polemic against the Sermon on the Mount and criticism of Jesus himself.[87]

Harnack makes a broader statement. He writes, "There is need of no more proof to establish that the gospel excludes all violence and has nothing in common with war and will not even permit it."[88] (Translated from German.)

Jesus Speaks Again

Perhaps the most popular text quoted in favor of the Christian serving the state in war has been: "Render . . . unto Caesar the things that are Caesar's . . ."[89] As such it must answer wholly the ethical problem of a Christian's relation to the state. But to use this passage in this way is to "beg the whole question."[90] Even a casual reading of the passage will drive one to the conclusion that the teaching of Christ in this passage is most indeterminate. An examination of it is necessary.

Jesus was teaching in the temple. The Jews were intent on entrapping Him for the purpose of destroying Him.[91] So the Pharisees, evidently at the behest of the Sanhedrin,[92] took counsel and contrived a question about one of the hottest Jewish political and religious issues. The question was whether it was permissible[93] for the Jews to pay the poll-tax, in short, to pay tribute to Rome.[94] The question which the disciples of the Pharisees propounded to Jesus was designed to incriminate Him irrespective of the way He might answer it. If Jesus would answer in the negative, He would fall under the displeasure of Rome. To make sure that the Roman authorities would know about such a verdict of Jesus, it seems the Herodians were invited to attend. If, however, Jesus would answer the query positively, the Jewish people would turn against Him.

The question is asked: "Is it lawful to give tribute unto Caesar, or not?" Jesus, exposing the evil character of the questioners, speaks: "Show me the tribute money." A denarius was brought to Him. The narrative goes on: "Whose is this image and superscription? They say unto him, Caesar's. Then saith he unto them, Render therefore unto Caesar the things that are Caesar's; and unto God the things that are God's."[95] They could not incriminate Him and so left Him.

It must be noticed first that Jesus spoke of the Jewish people, not as a theocracy, but as a subdued nation under a foreign power. It is clear from the teaching of Christ that He considered the unregenerate Jews as members of the "world" society and not as members of His kingdom.[96] Whatever Christ said to the Jews on this occasion, therefore, does not necessarily apply to the Christian as a member of an earthly state.

50

The answering of three questions will show the meaning of the statement of Christ in this passage. First, why did Jesus call for a coin and make His questioners acknowledge the image and superscription on it? Second, what did Christ mean with render, give back (*apodote*)? Third, what must be given back to Caesar and what must be given back to God?

It is most probable that Jesus wanted to point the Jews to the fact that they had, in effect, accepted the supremacy of Rome, when He made them acknowledge whose coinage they were using. With reference to this question, Strack and Biller-beck have the following significant statement to make: "that the realm of rulership of a king was co-extensive with the acceptance of his coinage, was commonly accepted as valid."[97] (Translated from German).

Another very probable reason for calling attention to the coin, which is actually an extension of the first, is well put by Swete, when speaking of the coin and its image:

The fact that it circulates in Judaea shews that in the ordering of God's providence Judaea is now under Roman rule; recognise facts, so long as they exist . . . and submit.[98]

Accepting this interpretation implies that Jesus was actually teaching subjection to the "powers that be." This would harmonize well with both Paul and Peter.

The parallel passages in the synoptics all have *apodote*. It must be noticed that Jesus changes the infinitive "to give" (*dounai*), which the questioners used, to render, "give back" (*apodote*). Since there is a variation in meaning in these two words, it is probable that Jesus purposely changed from the one the Jews used to the one with which He answered.

Thayer defines *apodidomi* (I give back) as "to give up, give over . . . deliver, relinquish . . . pay off, discharge . . . recompense . . ."[99] The implications are plain. The Jews possess something which is not their own. It belongs to Caesar.[100] This must be given back, repaid, relinquished. In paying taxes they simply relinquished that on which they had no claim or repaid that which had been given to them.

This introduces the final question on this passage. What must be given Caesar and what must be rendered to God? What the context clearly indicates is only the repayment as mentioned above. One seeks in vain for any other element which must be included in giving to Caesar. It is plain, therefore, that this verse will not admit of any interpretation which would suggest the rendering unto Caesar of any more than the poll-tax. This does not mean that the Jews or even the Christians must not render more. But it does mean that this verse does not teach that more is to be rendered. Paul Hutchinson saw this clearly when he remarked tersely, "All well and good, but the vital question remains: Who determines what is Caesar's and what is God's?"[101]

The same answer must be given with reference to repaying God. However, there seems to be one inference which, perhaps, was intended by Jesus in the second part of the answer to the Jews.

They were to give back to God what God had given them. The coin bore the image of Caesar, but they bore the image of God. They themselves were that which God had given.[102] They owed themselves to God. To give themselves back to God was their due to God. But the passage does not make this interpretation explicit. It must be regarded as an inference only.

To conclude, a few statements of summarization can be made. The political *status quo* was to be accepted.[103] Tribute to the Romans was to be paid. This, of course, shows that the Jews had obligations to Rome. But perhaps the greatest fact is that the Jews owed God themselves totally.

Another Passage

The "two swords" passage[104] is admittedly a difficult passage. Its meaning is obscure.[105] To determine its meaning three questions must be answered. First, for what purpose did Jesus

52

ask the disciples to buy swords? Again, what were these swords which the disciples present, and where did they come from?

The purpose which Jesus had in mind in calling for the swords could not have been defense. Even though Bruce, *et al.* do not accept a literal interpretation of this passage, yet he goes on to say that the two swords were enough for "one who did not mean to fight."[106]

First, it could not have been for the purpose of defense, for that would be contradictory to the teaching of submitting to persecution and His own example in suffering at His persecutor's hands. Second, it could not have been for defense because of the fact that any dependence upon the "arm of flesh" would have been totally useless. Again, when Peter used a sword at the time Christ was arrested, Christ forbade Peter to use it. Not only this, but He immediately undid by a miraculous act the violence which Peter had effected. Fourth, defense was not needed because Christ told Peter that legions of angels were at His disposal, if He desired defense.[107] Fifth, the very purpose for which Christ knew He was to be judged, condemned, and crucified evinces that Christ would not call for swords in defense of Himself. Sixth, it is clear from the record that Christ considered two swords to be enough. This conclusion is evident irrespective of how "it is enough" is interpreted.[108] This points to quite another purpose than defense of His person. Two swords could not have been enough for defense. Seventh, Christ specifically told Pilate that His disciples would not fight because of the nature of His kingdom.[109]

It seems that the reason for calling for the swords must be found in a figurative interpretation, left without answer, or found in a literal interpretation other than one which demands the reason to be the defense of Christ or His disciples.

A study of the context of the passage in Luke makes the latter approach possible. The central issue in this passage is clearly the swords. Accepting "For" (*gar*) as explanatory[110] of the central idea of the preceding verses[111] makes the prophecy in verse thirty-seven the reason for asking for the swords. For Christ and the disciples to carry the swords while meeting the multitude which was to come to Christ would lay them open to the charge that they were transgressors.

There is the further problem of where the disciples got the swords which they, seemingly immediately, presented to Christ. Bruce, in his commentary on Luke, asks this pointed question: "How did such a peaceable company come to have even so much as one sword?"[112]

It is evident from the passages that the disciples did not go to buy them. They must have been present in the upper room. Either the disciples carried them or they were simply in the room. It has been suggested that sword (*machaira*) is both a weapon and also a large knife "used for killing animals and cutting up flesh."[113] Wallace suggests that this tool was carried "by travellers, and often by peasants, [and] served several purposes; as jack-knife, hunting knife, butcher knife, pruning knife . . ." It was used in defense and war.[114] It has also been suggested that priests and the pacifistic Essenes carried these knives.[115] In connection with this it has been pointed out that the paschal lamb had been prepared in the upper room by two disciples. This would then suggest that the two knives were present because they had been used in preparing the Supper. At best these suggestions are only probabilities.

The only conclusion which can be drawn from this discussion is that the purpose of Jesus in asking for swords had no connection with violence, self-defense, or bloodshed. His purpose was to fulfill the Scriptures.

Peter's impetuous conduct in Gethsemane, when he used the sword which, seemingly, he was carrying, was an effort to defend his Master.[116] It is Jesus' words and action, as a result of Peter's act of violence, that merit examination here.

Bruce suggests that the sword which Peter carried was perhaps one of the two which were shown Christ in the upper room, and that it was perhaps the large knife used in connection with the paschal feast.[117] It is interesting to note that Peter carried one of these; for he was one of those in charge of preparing the passover feast.[118]

The basic fact in Christ's answer to Peter's action is that He flatly forbids Peter to use the sword, or knife, in violence. In contrast to this act by Peter, Jesus heals the wound which Peter inflicted. Peter was not even to resist on behalf of the one whom he loved most.

But the inquiry cannot be left there and the application made. What was Christ's purpose in forbidding the use of the sword? In the first place, Christ shows that it is unnecessary to use the sword because the powers of heaven are at His disposal. From this statement of Christ and His saying in John that He must drink "the cup" which God had given Him,[119] it is plain that Peter's act was forbidden because of Christ's immediate purpose of dying on the cross. It is therefore totally a matter of the will of God. This deduction is clear.

However, Jesus adds another statement which gives further reason for forbidding Peter the defense of Christ's person, in an aphoristic statement: "for all they that take the sword shall perish with the sword."[120] It seems to mean that Peter, or any of His disciples, were not to "take" the sword because this would involve them in the vicious circle of cause and effect of violence and hatred. Robertson, in a rather far-reaching application of the rebuke to Peter and this aphorism, has this to say:

Turn back thy sword into its place. It was a stern rebuke for Peter who had misunderstood the teaching of Jesus in Luke 22:38 as well as in Matt. 5:39 (cf. John 18:36). The reason given by Jesus had had innumerable illustrations in human history. The sword calls for the sword. Offensive war is here given flat condemnation.[121]

Perhaps Robertson is largely correct. But he has made one serious error. Peter's act was not an act of offense. It was strictly an act of defense.[122] Following Robertson's argument with this clear fact in mind makes both personal and national defense unlawful. This conclusion may be correct, and the aphorism as such may have this application. However, the forbidding was done to Peter as a disciple of Christ. If a broader view than the immediate purpose of Christ's suffering is taken, it would be best to apply the teaching of Christ as forbidding defense to the Christian brotherhood.

In the Gospel of John.—Three times in Jesus' pre-passion discourse with His disciples He used the phrase "the prince of the world" (*ho archon tou kosmou*), or its equivalent.[123] The evident concept behind this phrase is so closely allied with the conclusions drawn from the record of Jesus' temptation that a brief examination is in order.

The exegetes are largely agreed that *archon* here means ruler and that it is spoken of Satan. Robertson, taking this view, relates the concept expressed by Jesus to the claim of Satan in the temptation event. He says,

This phrase here, is descriptive of Satan as in possession of the evil world . . . In the temptations Satan claims power over the world and offers to share it with Jesus . . . Jesus did not deny Satan's power then, but here proclaims final victory over him.[124]

Thayer paraphrases this statement thus: ". . . the ruler of the irreligious mass of mankind . . ."[125]

Accepting the fact that Satan is characterized as the ruler of the world in these passages the examination must be focused on the questions which will determine the relevance of this rulership to the general problem of the Christian to the state. Two questions must find answers from the Scriptures. When is Satan the ruler of the "world?" What is meant by the "world?"

The inference from Christ's statement and the conclusion from the temptation event show plainly that at the time of the statement Satan was regarded by Jesus as the "ruler of the world." But now Jesus says, "now shall the prince of this world be cast out," (*nun . . . ekblethesetai*). The verb is the future passive of "cast out" (*ekballo*). The verb together with "now" (*nun*) evidently refer this act to the sacrificial death of Christ. This was to be the victory over Satan.[126] However, while the victory over Satan was procured in Christ's redemptive act,[127] the realization of this expulsion of Satan was not accomplished by Christ at His death.[128] That the rule of Satan over the world, factually, did not cease at Christ's death is clear from the writings of the apostles. Paul mentioned the relation of Satan to the world incidentally when he showed the Ephesians the spiritual nature of the forces opposing the Christian. His concept is clearly identical to the one Christ expressed in the phrase "the prince of the world" (*ho archon tou kosmou*). He says, ". . . our wrestling is . . . against the world-rulers of this darkness . . ."[129] He also calls Satan the god of this age, or world (*ho theos tou aionos toutou*).[130] These two expressions of Paul are evidently parallel.[131] John's concept was similar when he wrote, ". . . the whole world lieth in the evil one" (*kai ho kosmos holos en to ponero keitai*).[132]

There are two more lines of thought which parallel the concept of the continued rulership of Satan over the world which have direct bearing on this problem. Christ claims complete authority, received from the Father, "in heaven and in earth."[133] But this authority will not find ultimate realization until the consummation.[134] Satan himself is included in the final putting down of Christ's authority.[135]

The other line of thought is based on the concept of the nature of Satan's world rulership. The Scriptures conceive of Satan's rulership in the world as being effected by man's "service of sin . . ." It is thus that "he turns men's hearts according to his will."[136] Paul's concept is precisely this.[137] John follows the same view in his concept of "children of the devil."[138] This means that Satan's rulership is chronologically co-extensive with unregenerate mankind.

These considerations anticipate the meaning of "world" (*kosmos*). *Kosmos* with moral connotations is often used in the New Testament. John's and Paul's usages need only be examined for the purpose of this section. The epitome of its meaning can best be given by a quotation from Sasse.

First, of Paul's usage he writes, "The *kosmos* is the sum total of God's creation which has been ruined by the Fall and stands under the judgment of God, in which Jesus Christ appears as Saviour."[139] (Translated from German.)

The fullest concept is to be found in John, although Paul and John are in total agreement.[140]

When in John the *kosmos* is spoken of that it does not acknowledge God; that it does not believe; that it hates, it means that the *kosmos* must be understood as having personality attributes and is the great antagonist of the Savior in redemption history. It is to a certain degree a violent (*gewaltige*) collective person, which is represented by the *archon tou kosmou toutou* [prince of this world] . . . As those who believe in Christ are *en Christo* [in Christ], so the unbelieving *kosmos* [world] is *en to ponero* [in the evil one], and as Christ is *en humin* [in him], so is *archon tou kosmou toutou* [the prince of this world], *ho poneros*, the evil one *en to kosmou* [in the world] . . .[141] (Translated from German.)

In this definition, Paul's "saints" and John's "believers" are not of the world.[142]

Accepting this view of "world" as used here by Christ and the meaning of Satan's rule makes it plain that the Jewish world is as much under the sway of evil as the Gentile world.[143]

It must be concluded, therefore, that the total, sinful society, conceived of as being outside of Jesus Christ and His kingdom, is in a real and present sense under the rulership of Satan. It is this concept which enables one to understand the movements of history to modern times—violence, bloodshed, injustice, the raging of evil men. And the state must be conceived as part of and co-extensive with this society. Satan offered Christ the "kingdoms" of the world. This he could only do because they were his. Only thus was Christ's temptation a reality as recorded in Matthew and Luke.

Some modern thinkers, in their analyses of history, have looked "realistically" at the state and society and have come out with similar conclusions, and as Brunner remarks, "The state cannot be governed and ought not to be governed by love . . ."[144] Reinhold Niebuhr shows that the best of modern states are saturated by anti-Christian attitudes and policies when he shows how one of Britain's most noble statesmen committed the whole nation to war, in a speech, simply to maintain the British "honor."[145] Writing in a similar vein he says, "The dishonesty of nations is a necessity of political policy . . ."[146]

Speaking of the "official" ethic and Christianity, Heering gives the following position of Naumann: ". . . Naumann goes a step further on the path of honesty than is customary with the dominant official ethic, and explains that this political morality is not semi-Christian, or even relatively Christian, but wholly pagan."[147] Cadman quotes Viscount Morley as saying that "the political spirit is the great force in throwing love of truth and accurate reasoning into secondary place . . ."[148] Of international affairs with reference to war and peace, Reinhold Niebuhr ventures to say that peace gained by force is always "an unjust one."[149] The correlation between the concept which lies behind "the prince of this world" (*ho archon tou kosmou*), the nature of the state and the development of history, including present events, is too real to be dismissed.

At Christ's Trial

When Jesus was on trial before Pilate, He made two statements which must be discussed. The first one to be discussed is the famous statement of Jesus which reads, "My kingdom is not of this world: if my kingdom were of this world, then would my servants fight, that I should not be delivered to the Jews: but now is my kingdom not from hence."[150]

In dealing with Peter's violent action, with the purpose of defending his Master, it was concluded that Christ gave two reasons for forbidding Peter this action. One was the purpose for which Christ had come into the world. He said that He was going to drink the cup which His Father had given Him to drink. The second reason was because of the involvement of the Christian in violence and hatred and therefore sin, which violent defense must always bring.

In this passage, "The action of Peter is . . . again disavowed."[151] In this disavowal a further, more basic and far-reaching reason for forbidding Peter to use the sword is given. Jesus does not now say that His servants do not fight because of His purpose to redeem mankind. He says, rather, His servants do not fight because His kingdom is not of [out of] this world (*ek tou kosmou toutou*)." The preposition *ek*, according to Westcott, carries the force of origin and therefore points to the nature of the thing, in this case Christ's kingdom, thus originated.[152] This means that since the kingdom to which Christ refers as His own does not have its origin in the world (*kosmos*), it therefore does not partake of the nature and character of the *kosmos*. It "does [not] derive . . . its support from earthly forces . . ."[153] The nature and the character of the kingdom, therefore, and not His purpose to die, are here given by Jesus as the reason for not using violent coercion so that He would ". . . not be delivered to the Jews."[154]

Hoskyns puts it forcefully. He says,

The nature of His sovereignty corresponds with the nature of His mission. He is the king of Truth and He manifests His royal power not by force . . . His loyal subjects are therefore not those who fight, but those who, being of the Truth, obey their king."[155]

The nature and character of the kingdom, then, is the nature and character of the king. Therefore, the love that was commanded to be practiced, which was necessarily nonresistant, as seen in the Sermon on the Mount, is the character and nature of this kingdom. Christ clearly showed in the Sermon on the Mount that God at present does not directly resist evil and sin. His love causes equal treatment of the "just and the unjust." This passage which was spoken to Pilate is an enunciation of a universal as it pertains to the subjects of the kingdom. The whole concept of "new birth," regeneration, shows that the nature of the kingdom must be the nature of the subjects. Further, the "essential character of this kingdom is unchangeable."[156] It is therefore perfectly clear that Peter could take the nonresistance and love of Christ as revealed through the events of Christ's trial and crucifixion as absolute example for the Christians to follow even in the most serious persecution. Only if the attitude and the practice of Jesus were to be considered a universal for Christians would the Holy Spirit have permitted Peter to make the application which he did.[157]

It must be conceded, therefore, that this universal has more relevance to the Christian and the cause of Jesus Christ than its mere application to the direct employment of violence and coercion in the propagation of the gospel, and the work of the church. Rutenber points up the wider relevance of the application of this universal when he states:

. . . this becomes very relevant when efforts are made to sanctify a war by stressing the religious values that are at stake. We are told that the values of our Christian civilization were in the balance and that Hitler, for example, stood against everything we held dear. And all of this was true. But what is the conclusion? If we can neither propagate nor defend the cause of Christ and his kingdom—and here are our most precious treasures—by violence, is it probable that we are to defend the lesser values of our culture with it?[158]

This "my kingdom" passage has another pertinent angle to it. The guilt of Jesus, as conceived by the Jews, was in the realm of the religious. However, their charge is shifted to a political one as they confront Pilate with Jesus. The charge of blasphemy becomes the political charge of treason.[159] It is this charge which Jesus is answering Pilate in the passage under consideration.

The context, in John's Gospel, shows that Pilate cared nothing for the religious charge, but the political charge he was obliged to examine and so Pilate asks: ". . . Art thou the King of the Jews?"[160] The implication is that if Christ were, according to

61

Pilate's concept of kingship, He would oppose Rome. To this query Christ makes His famous answer.

The answer is clear. Caesar's kingdom is of this world. Christ's is not. Therefore, because of the nature and character of Jesus' kingdom, Caesar need not fear. Then Christ offers evidence for His answer. His servants do not seek to overthrow the "powers that be."[161] They are forbidden to use force or coercion to accomplish the establishment of Jesus' kingdom. The charge of treason, therefore, is without ground.

By this answer, Christ plainly affirms that He and His kingdom accept the political *status quo*. That is so, if it is accepted that the reason for Christ's conduct and His advice to the disciples is based on the nature and character of His kingdom and not on the expedients of the moment. A further conclusion which must be granted, if the above arguments are valid, is that this acceptance of the political *status quo* is co-extensive with Jesus' kingdom on earth. This means that the Christian, as a member of the kingdom, must accept the political *status quo* in any given state. The far-reaching significance of such conclusion can only be measured by an examination of the nature of the Roman state.

It was the Roman state which could perpetrate the grossest injustice of Christ's death. It was the Roman state, to which Jesus submitted, which was to be guilty of the unparalleled bloodshed of Christians.[162] It was a totalitarian state with a Caesar who claimed worship as deity. It was this state, with its political government which Christ accepted as the secular kingdom of the world. If Christ accepted this state and enjoined Christians to submit to it and not resist its evil, there is reason to conclude that all states regardless of their character must be included to which Christians are commanded to submit.

The other words of Jesus which He spoke during His trial before Pilate which must be discussed are found in the following chapter.[163] Jesus has been silent for a while. This seems to have vexed Pilate. He breaks out, with the evident motive of asserting his authority: "speakest thou not unto me" (*emoi ou laleis*), "knowest thou not that I have power to release thee, and have power to crucify thee?"[164] To this query comes the answer of Jesus, which must be examined now.

To determine the meaning of this statement of Christ to Pilate, there are three basic questions which must be answered. First, what is the meaning of authority (power) in this passage, and how is it related to Pilate and the act of condemning Jesus? Second, who are the persons or parties involved in the act of condemnation and how? Third, whose is the guilt which is committed in the act of condemnation and crucifixion?

It must be noticed that Pilate claims absolute freedom of will in exercising his authority in determining the fate of Jesus. Also, it is to be remembered that the question is not yet concerned with one or the other decision—releasing or crucifying Jesus. Both decisions will stand open before Pilate. Now Jesus does not deny that double authority which Pilate claims. He does, however, remind Pilate that that authority is from above, which must mean it comes from God.[165] Translating *kat' emou* as "regarding me," or "with reference to me,"[166] which seems more correct from the context than "against me," the answer of Jesus points to the fact that either decision can be made with the authority from God. The authority is Pilate's by virtue of constituted government.[167] "He therefore who exercises it is responsible, whatever he may suppose, to a higher power."[168] Pilate, here then, is not being used as a direct and irresponsible instrument by God to directly procure the death of His Son. With reference to this question Westcott says further: "It does not appear that there is . . . any reference to the fact that Pilate was an unconscious instrument of the divine will."[169] He adds, "That which 'was given,' it must be noticed, is not the authority itself, but the possession and exercise of it."[170]

There are two other factors which necessitate this interpretation. In the first place, if Pilate's authority had been given directly by God for the purpose to execute the death sentence on the Lord Jesus Christ, without Pilate by free will making the decision, it would mean that God himself is implicated in the guilt of murdering His own Son. This would be contrary to God's moral nature as revealed in His Word. Further, God is never blamed for the death of Christ. That sin is written to the account of evil men in the New Testament.[171]

The other factor is that Pilate is considered as being guilty in anticipation of his act of condemning Jesus in verse 11.[172] If he had been an irresponsible instrument in the hand of God, Pilate could have no guilt. The very nature of man's constitution makes this an impossibility.

The act of Pilate, therefore, is not the act of God. Pilate's act is an act of his free will working out God's purpose which in His foreknowledge God had determined must be done.[173]

But the historical event of Jesus' judgment and crucifixion has a much larger relation to personal beings than merely its relation to Pilate. In the first place, it was clearly the concept of Christ that there were evil "spiritual forces" at work in this historical event, which were seeking His destruction.[174] In the second place, there were men acting by their free will. In the third place, there was God. A few words must be said concerning God's role in this act of history.

It is one of the most obvious facts of revelation that the fact,[175] the time,[176], and the mode[177] of the death of Christ were foreordained in the foreknowing counsels of God. This means that in some way the hand of God was present in this act of history. However, as already shown, God could not have been directly an accomplice, and yet God's purpose was accomplished. A word of explanation is necessary.

First there is the revelation that God's determination of this event in history was according to His foreknowledge. There is one view of the foreknowledge of God which in no way interferes with the free will of man. This concept of fore-knowledge is here accepted. However, there is a second connection which God had with this event, which is seen clearly from events in the birth and life of Christ. Bearing in mind what God had purposed, there is evidence of God's restraining and withdrawing hand acting providentially in the events leading up to the death of Christ. First, there is the wrath of Herod. In his rage he seeks to kill Jesus. His violent hand is not stayed, but there is God's counter-move which thwarts his purpose.[178] Similar counter-moves are seen when the Jews would have killed Jesus before His "hour."[179] Jesus, as man, was subject to the cause and effect in the history of human society, and when these restraining acts of God ceased, evil men, motivated by their antagonism to God, acted of their own free choice and thus became guilty of the most immoral act of all history.

But the question is: How is the working out of God's purpose through the acts of sinful men possible? It is clear from the Scriptures and the foregoing considerations that God bears a twofold relation to the sinful acts of sinful men, with respect to His providential dealings with men. God restrains and permits sin. Of the latter relation, Strong says,

The decree to permit sin is . . . not an efficient but permissive decree, or a decree to permit, in distinction from a decree to produce by his own efficiency. No difficulty attaches to such a decree to permit sin, which does not attach to the actual permission of it.[180]

The decree to permit sin is a decree of creation[181] and therefore connected with the fundamental nature of man in his power of choice. But the providence of God in history, as outlined from Jesus' life, is more the act of not permitting, that is, of restraining, men from committing certain sinful acts.[182] In this relation of permitting and restraining exists the means by which God effects His purpose through the sinful acts of man. God bears other relations to events in history, but these are not important to the immediate problem.

In the historical act of condemning and crucifying Jesus there is, therefore, the concourse of the acts by three actors.

There are the Satanic forces. There is human society represented by instituted government acting by freedom of choice and God who has withdrawn His restraining hand. The outcome of this threefold concourse of acts has resulted in accomplishing the "determinate counsel and foreknowledge of God."[183]

If it is conceded that there is always the divine in history, as well as the human and the demonic, then there is no reason to deny that the analysis here made is true concerning all human history. This concession is here assumed.

If it be objected that this was a unique case in history and that therefore its relevance to all history is diminished, then it must be said that moral acts, as these were, are always basically the same; as also are justice and injustice. It is only the magnitude, or degree, of a moral act which is different, and not the kind.

There are, therefore, a few significant conclusions which can be drawn. First, the voice of government, or state, is not the voice of God, nor is the act of government the direct act of God. Second, the state in its governmental capacity is an instrument in the hand of God, but its acts in history are not irresponsible. They are fully responsible acts. If this conclusion were not correct, the fact of human government would constitute a travesty on the ultimate justice of God and impugn His moral character. The third conclusion which can be drawn is that a state is not ultimately authoritative. Absolute authority is in the hands of God.

The final question in the discussion of the words of Jesus is the question of guilt with reference to His death.[184] That sin and guilt are involved in causing Christ's death cannot be questioned. But this is the question: To whom does this guilt belong?

Jesus shows clearly that sin is involved. The idea of guilt is attached to Christ's usage of the word—sin.[185] Jesus also makes a comparison between the attachment of greater or lesser guilt to the parties involved. It seems that the party which delivered Christ to Pilate was "Caiaphas, the personal representative of 'the Jews' . . ."[186] Westcott then goes on to make the comparison apply to Caiaphas and Pilate, he says,

. . . the High-Priest . . . was more guilty. Pilate was guilty in using wrongfully his civil power. The High-Priest was doubly guilty, both in using wrongfully a higher (spiritual) power and in transgressing his legitimate rules of action.[187]

Both parties, therefore, have guilt. The High-Priest, together with the Sanhedrin, considered as functionaries of the Roman government since their courts were sanctioned by the Romans,[188] have guilt. Pilate, acting as the magistrate, also has guilt. Further, it is clear that it is personal guilt which is involved. Evidently, Jesus knows of no transfer of personal guilt to the state. That is, personal guilt is involved in spite of the fact that they were acting in official capacities. A further significant commentary on this problem is the prayer of Jesus on the cross when he prayed for the soldiers.[189] His prayer shows that Jesus attached personal guilt to their actions, otherwise, His prayer would have no meaning.

Moreover, one seeks in vain for Scripture to suggest the possibility of a personal sinful act becoming the guilt of society as a corporate whole, and the perpetrator of that act being by this transfer absolved. Further the principle of ultimate judgment and justice can have no meaning if the ultimate responsible entity is not that total personality which commits the act. The whole principle of justice and judgment is based on the concept of the individual, otherwise justice must go by default.

That the Scriptures cannot contain both the teaching of "private" and "official" morality seems further evident when one considers the concept realistically. Luther has portrayed the true meaning of this position. Macgregor quotes from Luther's *Ob Kriegsleute auch in seligem Stande sein koennen*:

'The hand which bears such a sword (the sword of government) is as such no longer man's hand but God's; and not man it is, but God, who hangs, breaks on the wheel, beheads, strangles and wages war . . . It is not I that smites, thrusts and kills, but God and my Prince, whose servants are my hand and life.'[190]

Troeltsch remarks tersely, "The Protestant way out of the strain of a dual morality, personal and official, is not a solution, but a reformulation of the problem."[191]

Jesus' Example

Its relation to the subject.—Christ's attributes of deity and moral perfection remained unchanged in His incarnation.[192] This means that there can be no moral discrepancy between His teaching and His life.

Further, the Scriptures present Christ as the absolute moral example for the Christian to follow. This is borne out by two factors. First, the nature of regeneration shows that it is a work of conforming to "the image of his Son."[193] The second factor is the specific teaching of the Scriptures making Christ the supreme example for the Christian.[194] This teaching is especially significant because it takes the very acts of Christ as he was on trial and going to the cross as that example for Christians.

The cleansing of the Temple.[195]—This incident in Christ's life is discussed because it is often used in attempts to qualify the Saviour's teaching of nonresistance.[196] It is alleged that Jesus used violence in the "expulsion" of the sellers and money changers from the temple.

First it must be recognized that "cast out" (*ekballo*) does not necessarily suggest the use of force. The Greek word is at times translated as "send forth."[197] It is used by Peter to send friends out of a room.[198] It is most often used by Jesus on the casting out of demons.[199] Factually, there are only some two or three usages where physical force is necessarily meant.[200]

Of the act of driving out, Robertson shows that *ekballo* applies only to the sheep and cattle. Even here he doubts that Jesus actually used the whip made of rope upon the cattle and sheep for "a flourish of the scourge would answer."[201]

It must therefore be concluded that there is no evidence in this passage that any coercion was used. It was the forceful command of the Master and His august presence which expelled the men from the court of the temple.

His general example.—A few quotations present a summary of Jesus' example.

Macgregor speaks on nonresistance:

Though He consistently lived by a principle of "nonresistance," yet there was nothing negative about His life. He never belittled or condoned the stark reality of evil; but He never met it with its own methods and weapons. He overcame evil with good.[202]

On Jesus' relation to the state, Leiper says,

Jesus met . . . a conflict of loyalties and obeyed God rather than men. Yet he did not discredit the importance of government nor refuse to pay taxes or to obey legal authority in all ordinary circumstances.[203]

E. Scott remarks thus:

In his own behavior, Jesus was duly observant of all civic laws and ordinances. At the trial it was found impossible to produce any real evidence against him as a disturber of public order . . . Throughout his teaching he assumes that men ought to submit to constituted authority . . .[204]

And yet it is also true ". . . that He acted in total independence of the State all through His ministry . . ."[205]

Cadoux sums up the example of Jesus in one sentence. He says, ". . . his *own* conduct throughout corresponds closely with the injunctions he gave to them."[206]

FOOTNOTES

[1]Matt. 4:1-11.
[2]Luke 4:1-13.
[3]Matt. 4:8.
[4]Cf. John 2:24, 25.
[5]Luke 4:6.

⁶Lewis Sperry Chafer, *Systematic Theology* (Dallas: Dallas Seminary Press, 1948), VII, 177 f.; W. Robertson Nicoll, *The Expositor's Greek New Testament* (London: Hodder and Stoughton, n.d.), I 90 f.

⁷Bernhard Weiss, *Biblical Theology of the New Testament,* trans. David Eaton (3d ed. rev.; Edinburgh T. & T. Clark, 1882), I, 104.

⁸*"basileia,"* A *Greek-English Lexicon of the New Testament,* trans. Joseph Henry Thayer (rev. enlarged ed., New York: American Book Company, 1889).

⁹*"oikoumene," ibid.*

¹⁰Archibald Thomas Robertson, *Word Pictures in the New Testament* (New York: Harper & Brothers, 1930), I, 33.

¹¹Matt. 5:38-48.

¹²Cf. Heinrich August Wilhelm Meyer, *Critical and Exegetical Hand-Book to the Gospel of Matthew,* trans. Peter Christie (ed. and rev.; New York: Funk and Wagnalls Company, 1884), p. 136.

¹³Matt. 5:38; cf. Exod. 21:24; Lev. 24:20; Deut. 19:21.

¹⁴Hermann Olshausen, *Biblical Commentary on the New Testament,* trans. (rev. from 4th German ed.; New York: Shelden & Company, Publishers, 1866), I, 312 ff.

¹⁵Meyer, *op. cit.,* p. 136.

¹⁶Matt. 5:43-48.

¹⁷Matt. 5:1, 2; cf. Luke 6:20.

¹⁸Matt. 5:13, 18, et **cetera.**

¹⁹Matt. 5:11, 13, 14; 6:8-15; 7:11.

²⁰Hans Windisch, *The Meaning of the Sermon on the Mount,* trans. S. Maclean Gilmour (Philadelphia: The Westminster Press, 1937), p. 171.

²¹Rom. 12:14-21.

²²Matt. 28:20a.

²³Olshausen, *op. cit.,* I, 313.

²⁴Windisch, *op. cit.,* p. 107.

²⁵Cf. Chafer, *op. cit.,* V, 113 f.

²⁶Cf. Matt. 5:29, 30.

²⁷Windisch, *op. cit.,* pp. 24 ff.

²⁸Matt. 5:38-48.

²⁹Exod. 21:24; Lev. 24:20; Deut. 19:22.

³⁰Cf. Exod. 21:22; Cf. Lev. 24:13-20; Cf. Deut. 19:17-21.

³¹Cf. W. F. Adeney (ed.), *The Century Bible — St. Matthew* (rev. ed.; Edinburgh: T. C. and E. C. Jack, Ltd., n.d.), p. 121.

³²Nicoll, *op. cit.,* I, 111 f.

³³Lev. 24:19.

³⁴Exod. 21:18-20.

³⁵Exod. 21:35, 36.

³⁶Deut. 19:19b-21.

[37]Lev. 19:18.

[38]Shrenk, *"ekdikesis,"* *Theologisches Woerterbuch zum Neuen Testament,* ed. Gerhard Kittel, Vol II (1950).

[39]Alvah Hovey (ed.), *An American Commentary on the New Testament,* (Philadelphia: American Baptist Publication Society, 1886), p. 117: Cf. Herman Strack and Paul Billerbeck, *Kommentar zum Neuen Testament aus Talmud und Midrasch* (Muenchen: C. H. Beck'she Verlagsbuchhandlung, 1922), I, 341 f.

[40]Windisch, *op. cit.,* pp. 31 f.

[41]Henry Alford, *The Greek New Testament* (3 ed.; New York: Harper and Brothers, 1959), I, 46.

[42]Cf. I Pet. 5:8, 9.

[43]Matt. 5:44.

[44]Cf. Matt. 23.

[45]John 18:8.

[46]John 7:1, 10; 10:39. Cf. Luke 4:30.

[47]Albert C. Knudson, *The Principles of Christian Ethics* (New York: Abingdon-Cokesbury Press, 1943), p. 231.

[48]Hovey, *Commentary on the Gospel of Matthew,* p. 118.

[49]Matt. 24, et cetera, also Isa. 18-1-10.

[50]Nicoll, *op. cit.,* I, 111.

[51]Matt. 13:29, 30, 33-43; 25:31-46; 24:5-14; et cetera.

[52]Matt. 24:7.

[53]Cf. Merrill F. Unger, *Biblical Demonology* (2d ed.; Wheaton: Van Kampen Press, Inc., 1953), p. 188.

[54]Rom. 13:1-7.

[55]I. Pet. 2:11-15.

[56]Cf. Terry, *op. cit.,* p. 416.

[57]Brunner, *The Divine Imperative,* p. 229.

[58]Matt. 5:39b.

[59]Hovey, *Commentary on the Gospel of Matthew,* p. 118.

[60]*Ibid.,* p. 119.

[61]Matt. 5:40.

[62]Hovey, *op. cit.,* p. 118.

[63]Nicoll, *op. cit.,* I, 112.

[64]Matt. 5:41.

[65]Alford, *op. cit.,* I, 46.

[66]Matt. 5:42.

[67]Matt. 5:43.

[68]Strack and Billerbeck, *op. cit.,* I, 353.

[69]Matt. 5:44.

[70]Matt. 5:43.

[71]Matt. 5:44.

[72]Meyer, *Critical and Exegetical Hand-Book on the Gospel of Matthew*, p. 138.

[73]Strack and Billerbeck. *op. cit.*, I, 353 f.

[74]Alford, *op. cit.*, I, 47.

[75]Nicoll, *op. cit.*, I, 114.

[76]William Evans, "Love," *The International Standard Bible Encyclopedia*, Vol. III (1949).

[77]Cf. I Cor. 13; Rom. 12:20, 21; 13:10.

[78]Rom. 12:19, 20.

[79]J. R. Coates (trans. and ed.), *Bible Key Words from Gerhard Kittel's Theologisches Woerterbuch zum Neuen Testament* (New York: Harper & Brothers, Publishers, 1951), pp. 48 f.

[80]Matt. 5:48.

[81]Cf. James 4:17; Rom. 6:1 ff.

[82]Cf. II Thess. 1:7-9, et cetera.

[83]Brunner, *Justice and the Social Order*, p. 129.

[84]Rutenber, *op. cit.*, p. 76.

[85]Meyer, *Critical and Exegetical Hand-Book on the Gospel of Matthew*, p. 138; cf. Brunner, *The Divine Imperative*, pp. 222 ff.

[86]Niebuhr, *Christianity and Power Politics*, p. 30.

[87]Windisch, *op. cit.*, p. 172.

[88]Harnack, *op. cit.*, p. 2.

[89]Matt. 22:21; Mark 12:17; Luke 20:25; Rutenber, *op. cit.*, p. 29.

[90]*Ibid.*, p. 30.

[91]Luke 20:19, 20.

[92]Matt. 22:15; cf. Luke 20:19 and Mark 11:27; cf. Willoughby C. Allen, *A Critical and Exegetical Commentary on the Gospel According to St. Matthew* ("The International Critical Commentary"; New York: Charles Scribner's Sons, 1913), p. 237.

[93]Hovey, *Commentary on the Gospel of Matthew*, p. 452.

[94]*Ibid.*

[95]Matt. 22:17-21.

[96]John 3:1 ff.

[97]Strack and Billerbeck, *op. cit.*, I, 884.

[98]Henry Barclay Swete, *The Gospel According to St. Mark* (3d ed.; London: Macmillan and Co., Ltd., 1909), p. 276.

[99]"*apodidomi*," *A Greek-English Lexicon of the New Testament.*

[100]Cf. A. T. Robertson, *A Grammar of the Greek New Testament in the Light of Historical Research* (Nashville: Broadman Press, 1934), p. 767.

[101]Hutchinson, *op. cit.*, p. 34.

[102]Cf. Hovey, *Commentary on the Gospel of Matthew*, pp. 453 f.

[103]Walter Kuenneth, *Politik zwischen Daemon und Gott* (Berlin: Lutherisches Verlagshaus, 1954), p. 34.

[104]Luke 22:35-38.

[105]Cf. Alfred Plummer, *A Critical and Exegetical Commentary of the Gospel According to St. Mark* (10th ed., "The International Critical Commentary"; New York: Charles Scribner's Sons, 1914), pp. 506 f.

[106]Nicoll, *op. cit.*, I, 629.

[107]Matt. 26:53.

[108]Luke 22:38.

[109]John 18:36.

[110]Cf. Robertson, *A Grammar of the Greek New Testament in the Light of Historical Research, pp.* 1190 f.

[111]Cf. Luke 22:35-38.

[112]Nicoll, *op. cit.*, I, 629.

[113]*"machaira," A Greek-English Lexicon of the New Testament.*

[114]James Wallace, *Fundamentals of Christian Statesmanship* (New York: Fleming H. Revell Company, 1939), p. 294.

[115]*Ibid.,* p. 295.

[116]Matt. 26:51-54. Cf. John 18:10, 11; also Luke 22:48.

[117]Nicoll, *op. cit.*, I, 317.

[118]Luke 22:7, 8.

[119]John 18:11.

[120]Matt. 26:52.

[121]Robertson, *Word Pictures in the New Testament,* I, 216.

[122]Rutenber, *op. cit.*, p. 39.

[123]John 12:31; 14:30; 16:11.

[124]Robertson, *Word Pictures in the New Testament,* V, 228 f.

[125]*"archon," A Greek-English Lexicon of the New Testament.*

[126]Robertson, *Word Pictures in the New Testament,* V, 229.

[127]Col. 2:15.

[128]Cf. Heinrich August Wilhelm Meyer, *Critical and Exegetical Hand-Book to the Gospel of John,* trans. Frederick Crombie (rev. ed.; New York: Funk & Wagnalls Company, 1884), p. 375.

[129]Eph. 6:12 (ASV).

[130]II Cor. 4:4.

[131]John Peter Lange, *The Gospel According to John,* trans., rev., and ed. Philip Schaff ("A Commentary on the Holy Scriptures"; New York: Charles Scribner & Co., 1871), p. 387.

[132]I John 5:19. Cf. Robertson, *Word Pictures in the New Testament,* VI, 245.

[133]Matt. 28:18.

[134]Cf. I Cor. 15:24-26, and Rev. 20:7-15.

[135]Cf. Henry Barclay Swete, *The Apocalypse of St. John* (3d ed.; London: Macmillan and Co., Ltd., 1909), p. 270.

[136]Weiss, *op. cit.*, I, 104.

[137]Eph. 2:2.

[138]I John 3:6-10.

[139]Sasse, *"kosmos," Theologisches Woerterbuch zum Neuen Testament,* Vol. III.

[140]*Ibid.*

[141]*Ibid.*

[142]*Ibid.*

[143]Alvah Hovey (ed.), *Commentary on the Gospel of John* ("An American Commentary on the New Testament"; Philadelphia: American Baptist Publication Society, 1886), p. 256.

[144]Brunner, *The Divine Imperative,* p. 462.

[145]Niebuhr, *Moral Man and Immoral Society,* pp. 92 f.

[146]*Ibid.,* p. 95.

[147]Heering, *op. cit.,* pp. 106 f.

[148]S. Parkes Cadman, *Christianity and the State* (New York: The Macmillan Company, 1924), p. 31.

[149]Niebuhr, *Moral Man and Immoral Society,* p. 19.

[150]John 18:36.

[151]Edwyn Clement Hoskyns, *The Fourth Gospel,* ed. Francis Noel Davey (London: Faber and Faber, Ltd., 1947), p. 520.

[152]Lange, *The Gospel According to St. John,* p. 565.

[153]B. F. Wescott, *The Gospel According to St. John* (London: John Murray, 1882), p. 260.

[154]John 18:36.

[155]Hoskyns, *op. cit.,* pp. 520 f.

[156]Cf. Lange, *The Gospel According to St. John,* p. 565.

[157]I Pet. 2:21-23.

[158]Rutenber, *op. cit.,* pp. 39 f.

[159]H. D. A. Major, T. W. Manson, and C. J. Wright, *The Mission and Message of Jesus* (New York: E. P. Dutton and Co., Inc., 1947), p. 918. Cf. Luke 23:2.

[160]John 18:33.

[161]Cf. Lange, *The Gospel According to St. John,* p. 565.

[162]Schaff, *op. cit.,* I, 380 ff.

[163]John 19:11.

[164]John 19:10.

[165]J. H. Bernard, *A Critical and Exegetical Commentary on the Gospel According to St. John* ("The International Critical Commentary": New York: Charles Scribner's Sons, 1929), II, 620.

[166]Cf. Robertson, *A Grammar of the Greek New Testament in the Light of Historical Research,* p. 607.

[167]Cf. Westcott, *op. cit.,* p. 270.

[168]*Ibid.*

[169]*Ibid.*, p. 271.

[170]*Ibid.* Note: Westcott points out that the participial construction is: *"Endedomenon"* and not *"Endedomene."*

[171]Acts 2:23; 3:14, 15; 4:25-28; 7:52.

[172]John 19:11.

[173]Acts 2:23; 4:25-28.

[174]John 14:20; cf. Luke 22:31, 32; Col. 2:5.

[175]Isa. 53; Acts 2:23; 4:27, 28.

[176]John 2:4; 7:8; 8:20; 17:1.

[177]Ps. 22; Acts 4:27, 28.

[178]Matt. 2:12-15.

[179]Luke 4:30; John 7:1, 10; 10:39.

[180]Augustus Hopkins Strong, *Systematic Theology* (Philadelphia: Griffith Rowland Press, 1909), p. 365.

[181]Cf. *Ibid.*, p. 353.

[182]Cf. Kuenneth, *op. cit.*, p. 46.

[183]Acts 2:22, 23.

[184]Cf. Bernard, *op. cit.*, II, 620.

[185]Cf. John 19:11.

[186]Westcott, *op. cit.*, p. 271.

[187]*Ibid.*, pp. 270 f.

[188]Paul Levertoff, "Sanhedrin," *The International Standard Bible Encyclopedia*, IV, 2688 ff. John 18:31.

[189]Luke 23:34.

[190]Macgregor, *op. cit.*, p. 130.

[191]Troeltsch, *op. cit.*, II, 509.

[192]II Cor. 5:21; Col. 1:19; 2:9; Heb. 4:15; I Pet. 2:22.

[193]Rom. 8:29; Col. 3:10; II Pet. 1:4.

[194]I Pet. 2:20-25.

[195]John 2:13-17.

[196]Cf. Hershberger, *op. cit.*, p. 356.

[197]Luke 10:2; Mark 1:43.

[198]Acts 9:40.

[199]Mark 1:34.

[200]Cf. *"ekballo,"* *The Englishman's Greek Concordance of the New Testament* (9th ed., London: Samuel Bagster and Sons, Ltd., 1908).

[201]Robertson, *Word Pictures in the New Testament*, V, 38.

[202]Macgregor, *op. cit.*, p. 47.

[203]Leiper, *op. cit.*, p. 100.

[204]Ernest F. Scott, *The Ethical Teaching of Jesus* (New York: The Macmillan Company, 1924), p. 79.

[205]Wallace, *op. cit.*, p. 310.

[206]Cecil John Cadoux, *Christian Pacifism Re-examined*, p. 85.

CHAPTER IV

PAUL AND THE CHRISTIAN'S RELATION TO THE STATE

Paul's Teaching

Introductory considerations.—The most elaborate and specific body of teaching in the New Testament on the Christian's relation to the state is Romans 13:1-7. However, it must be granted that this passage must be supplemented and the apparently absolute statements must be qualified by Paul's total ethical outlook and teaching. This fact is based on a principle which must govern all valid Bible exposition. We can state, therefore, with Nygren that the passage ". . . is part of his [Paul's] total theological outlook."[1] A few examples of how Paul's apparently absolute statements must be conditioned by his total view will help clarify this section.

To the Corinthians, Paul writes: "All things are lawful for me; but not all things are expedient."[2] A few verses previous to this statement, Paul has given the catalogue of gross sins.[3] The observation which must be made at this point is that Paul could not have made this statement without assuming that it was conditioned by his fundamental moral teaching.

Perhaps an even more striking example is found in another passage in the following chapter of Corinthians.[4] The apostle, in these verses, gives instruction to the Corinthians to remain in that "calling" in which they were when they were called

76

of the Lord, and states no qualifications. Was he indifferent to the morality or immorality involved in the "calling" of the converts? The answer must be an emphatic no. Evidently Paul assumed the application of all his ethical teaching to this seemingly absolute injunction. This method of Paul's writings must be remembered in the exegesis of Romans 13:1-7.

Paul's concept of the state as derived from Romans is often presented as optimistic and extremely favorable.[5] This view is rooted in the concept that human government is taught by Paul to be characterized by divinity. This is alleged to have been Paul's view because of the favorable treatment he had received from the Roman authorities till the time of writing the Roman letter.[6] If Paul had written, it is alleged, after the Neronian persecution he would not have written as he did.[7]

The time question will be discussed later. At this point Paul's general concept is considered. Paul's concept of "world" as relating to human government has been discussed. It was concluded that Paul conceived of human government as in a real way being dominated by demonic power.[8] His profound understanding of sinful human nature and its relation to the spirit-powers of evil[9] make this concept necessary. Paul could not have spoken of the "world rulers" (*kosmokratoras*),[10] referring to the evil spiritual powers which rule the "world," or of the god of this age (world) (*ho theous tou aionos toutou*)[11] if this had not been his concept. If Cullmann can be followed, there is another striking statement of Paul which bears directly and specifically on this concept. This statement of Paul was made considerably before he wrote Romans. Cullmann says,

In I Cor. 2:8 . . . Paul writes that the rulers of this world had not recognized this wisdom. 'For had they recognized it, they would not have crucified the Lord of glory.' By 'the rulers of this age' Paul manifestly means *both* the invisible 'princes of this world,' who are often mentioned as such, and their actual human instruments, Herod and Pilate.[12]

Finally, when the unity and divine inspiration of the New Testament are taken into consideration, the conclusion, that demonic forces are at work in world government, is inescapable. This concept must condition the exegesis in Romans chapter 13.

Another question must be answered. Did Paul's view change? As already shown, Paul's concept of the demonic in state government seems to be precisely the same before and after writing Romans. This is gathered from the distribution of the passages in his earlier and later letters dealing with the concept.

There is also no indication that Paul had changed his mind on the Christian's relation to the state. His epistles to Timothy are evidence of this. Accepting the dates of the writing of these letters, as given by Thiessen, makes both the first and second letter to Timothy and also Titus fall in the general period of the Neronian persecution.[13] It would seem, also, that Paul was convinced that he would be obliged to give his life at this time, evidently at the hand of the empire.[14]

In I Timothy and Titus, Paul repeats the injunction of submission to government and enjoins the Christian's obedience to magistrates and prayer for the authorities in government.[15] In the second letter to Timothy, even as he realizes that the Roman authorities were about to execute him, there is no retraction of previous injunctions concerning the Christian's attitude and relation to the Roman government, nor does one find any bitterness toward it.

It must be concluded, therefore, that Paul's teaching on the Christian's relation to the state is uniform throughout.[16] Paul did not change his mind; at least, the Biblical record admits of no such conclusion. These considerations would rather point to the view that what Paul taught he taught on principle. This is all the more evident when the teaching and example of Jesus is admitted to undergird Paul's teaching.

Lange and Fay have this to say on the subject:

In view of the universal character of this Epistle, even on its practical side, the Apostle must have felt the necessity of defining from his principle, the relation of duty in which Christians stood to the State, without his having been led to it by this or that circumstance.[17]

In conjunction with this, one word must be said of the view of Peter. In view of the impending clash with the Roman government during the Neronian rule,[18] Peter enjoins precisely the same general attitude and actions[19] as Paul and Jesus had enjoined. This points so strongly in the direction of teaching on principle rather than a teaching borne out of expedients and circumstances that it lends weight to the similar argument with reference to Paul.

In Romans.—As indicated, Romans 13:1-7 carries the burden of Paul's teaching on the Christian's relation to the state. What does Paul teach in this section? To arrive at an understanding there are four questions which must be answered. First, what is the purpose of giving this instruction? Second, of what states and their governments is Paul speaking; and does his teaching have universal significance or is it a concept which is temporary and significant only to the situation under which Paul finds himself at the time of writing? Third, what is God's relation to the state and government and what is therefore the nature of the state? Fourth, what is the Christian's relation to that state?

What seems pre-eminently clear from the context of the passage and the purpose of the Roman epistle is that Paul's central intention is not to present a theory of political government,[20] nor to write a pattern for the secular state, nor even to describe the true nature of a state, but rather to instruct a Christian community as to its attitude and obligation to the state. That Paul would touch on some aspects of the nature and function of the state is to be expected. However, these are incidental and so do not constitute the burden or the purpose for writing.

The occasion of writing these instructions may have had some connection with the Jewish tumult in Rome when the differentiation between Jews and Christians had not yet been clearly drawn by the Romans.[21] However, there are a number of reasons to believe that this body of teaching as has already been pointed out, was rather Paul's treatment of "the question from the viewpoint of moral principle, which always remains the standard for the Christian."[22]

The passage is closely related to its immediate context. Nygren sees in this passage a connection to Paul's theme of the whole practical section of Romans—"*in this aeon.*"[23] He thinks the question here is: "How should he [the Christian] shape his life in relation to the orders of this world?"[24]

There is also strong evidence that the passage on the state is not isolated material in that there is the contrast of the application of vengeance. In the last verses of chapter twelve, all vengeance, or the application of justice, is forbidden to the Christian. In chapter thirteen, Paul clearly shows that God's agency for vengeance and administration of what must be relative justice is the state.[25] There is also a similar carry-over of the theme of love.[26] Still another point which can be made is that Paul shows in these two chapters, the Christian's proper relation (1) to church community,[27] (2) to individual persons,[28] and (3) to the civil powers.[29] The unity of these chapters is therefore easily seen. The organic relation of Paul's teaching in these chapters points in the direction that his teaching was part of his whole outlook on the conduct of Christians, and for that reason he gave the specific teaching on the Christian and state.

One seems justified, therefore, to conclude with Nygren that, "He is not here giving casuistic counsels how his readers should act towards the authorities in different situations; he is setting forth the basic Christian view about worldly government."[30] This conclusion partly embraces what must be further examined in the text: With reference to what state can the teaching of Paul be applied?

Before proceeding it must be stated that, since there is apparently total agreement that Paul wrote about the state in its governmental function in this passage, no special discussion on this aspect of the text is presented. However, the words which are used to represent the government and its functionaries must be defined. The word to be defined at this point is power (authority), (exousia). Thayer defines exousia as "1. power of choice, liberty of doing as one pleases; leave or permission . . . 2. physical and mental power; the ability or strength with which one is endued, which he either possesses or exercises . . . 3. the power of authority . . . and of right . . . 4. the power of rule of government . . ."[31] It is plainly the last meaning which is meant by Paul in this passage. However, the concept of the power of choice is necessarily a part of the meaning when used with reference to government. As has been pointed out, it was this concept of the power of choice, precisely the power of judicial choice,[32] which was claimed by Pilate and of which he was reminded by Jesus that this authority came from God.[33] This latter concept is particularly important in the idea of governmental authority, as Paul conceived of it.[34]

The text must now be examined. Concerning what state or government is Paul writing? First, there is evidence in the text that its teaching is as timeless as the teaching of its context. This is shown by the fact that Paul had evidently taken up the instruction of Jesus to be submissive to Rome, which Christ also exemplified, and to give back to Rome what belongs to it.[35]

Second, it must be noticed that the language in the text also points to timeless principles. It is significant to notice that the first two times Paul writes "authority" he omits the article. The second of these statements goes on to define these powers. It seems as if Paul's mind immediately envisions a number of qualifications to the first statement that "every soul" should submit to governmental authorities, and so he reinforces his meaning of "authorities" by saying that no authority exists except "of God" (*hupo theou*). This negative universal statement he immediately undergirds with the positive side of the same argument. He says "the powers that be are ordained of God" (*hai de ousai hupo theou tetagmenai eisin*). This is also a universal statement which is the necessary obverse of the negative, if it is granted that authorities have existence. This must lead to the conclusion that *de facto* government is the government here meant.[36]

Shedd draws the same conclusion when he says that it

. . . denotes an 'actually existing' authority: a government de facto, though possibly not de jure, in all respects . . . the fact that a civil government is organized, and in actual operation, is an evidence that God has so appointed, in his providence. The plural implies that there are varieties in the forms of human government.[37]

As from the general considerations of the context of Romans 13:1-7, so also from the text itself, it can be concluded that Paul has laid down principles for the conduct of Christians in their relations to the state, which evince perpetual validity. They are valid under all circumstances and forms of state governments. In Paul's concept of government all human governments are therefore included.[38]

Another vital problem is that of God's relations to secular, human government, and therefore its nature and function. What does Paul teach on this problem in Romans? Paul has made three statements which bear directly on God's relation to human government. First, he says, that it is "of God" (*hupo theou*). Then he says that it is "ordained, or appointed by God" (*hupo theou tetagmenai*). And, again, he says that he who resists the authority resists "the ordinances, or order, of God" (*te tou theou diatage*). Each of these statements is still dealing with the abstract—"authority" (*exousia*).[39] "Of God" (*hupo theou*) shows that the source of authority is God. Although not much weight can be placed on the use of the preposition, yet it is to be noticed that "from" (*apo*), with partitive significance, is not used by Paul, rather, he uses "of" (hupo). This preposition has more the idea of efficient cause.[40] Basing his conclusions on other facts, Behm speaks of authority as being lent by God. He further suggests that even Satan's authority has been given him.[41] This is the only view compatible with the Christian denial of dualism. The words of Jesus, stating that all authority has been given Him in heaven and in earth,[42] must be understood with this implication in mind.

It can be concluded, therefore, that all human authority is derived authority and therefore not absolute, but circumscribed by the authority of God. Further, the transmission of authority does not include the transmission of moral character. The basic meaning of authority, as the power of choice, accords with this conclusion. The moral element in "authority" (ex-ousia) enters in the use of it and not in the possession of it. Therefore the fact that human government has derived its exousia from God says nothing about its moral character. Neither can it mean, therefore, that any element of the divine moral character is possessed by the state. [43] A realistic view of history clearly shows this to be true also. The moral character of any government or state is acquired by the use of its God-lent authority.[44]

Paul also says that de facto authorities are ordained (tetag-menai) of God. To emphasize the reason why the Christian must submit and not resist the state, Paul describes the authorities as the order or ordinance (diatage) of God. Both these Greek words have a common root—tasso. The meaning of these two words is similar. The words are also here used to describe the same fact. They can therefore be discussed together.

Thayer defines diatage as "a disposition, arrangement, ordinance . . ."[45] Tasso he defines thus: "to place in certain order . . . to arrange, to assign a place, to appoint . . ."[46]

Liddell and Scott give a few other angles of meaning to *tasso*. They put emphasis on the concept of appointing to service or assigning to a duty, both civil and military, or appointing to a task.[47]

The conclusion which must be drawn from Paul's usage of this word is that *de facto* human government is the arrangement of God. God has appointed it to perform a certain task. There is in these words no meaning which would imply divine character in human government because of the fact that it is the arrangement of God.[48] In making this statement, Paul does not take into account that there may be good or evil governments, or good or evil men in responsible positions.[49] That is not the question to Paul at the moment. Neither does Paul intimate by what method God has made the government his tool to perform his purpose. This question must be answered from other Scriptures or be left in the realm of the unsearchable counsels of God.[50]

From the abstract designations of human government, Paul passes on to the concrete. He uses three terms to designate the concrete and personal embodiment of the authority in the state. These are: *archontes*,[51] *diakonos*,[52] and *leitourgoi*.[53] In connection with these terms Paul sets forth functions of human government. The first term designates rulers,[54] pointing primarily to the relationship of ruling persons to the ruled. The second term means servant. Robertson takes it in a "general sense."[55] It is used for "power, authority" (*exousia*) in verse four and thus stands for the total aspect of rulership and government. It must be noticed that this term is used in a two-fold relationship. The government is God's servant—*diakonos*. And it is God's servant for the benefit of the Christian —"to thee for good" (*soi eis to agathon*).[56]

He also shows what constitutes this benefit for the Christian. It is that the state is God's minister for the purpose of avenging those which are practicing evil. That is, as has been pointed out, in dealing with the Sermon on the Mount, the administration of justice.[57]

For the term—*leitourgoi* (ministers)—verse six, Robertson gives a full meaning. He says it is a "Late word for public servant." It is plural and therefore speaks of the rulers as persons who are involved in the administration of government. It is

Often used of military servants, servants of the king, and temple servants (Heb. 8:2). Paul uses it also of himself as Christ's *leitourgos* (Rom. 15:16) and Epaphroditus as a minister to him (Phil. 2:25).[58]

And so Lenski concludes that to read into this word either a sacred or a pagan meaning is useless. It "applied to anyone who acts as a public servant in a public capacity."[59]

This word is also used in a twofold relationship. There is the God-ward and man-ward relationship." For again Paul says that these are God's servants, and adds that they are "attending continually upon this very thing." Relating the statement to verse four, and its proper antecedents, reveals the purpose for which the state is God's servant. Godet sums up and clarifies this purpose when he says that it is "to make justice reign by checking evil and upholding good."[60]

A word must be said about the function of the state as Paul conceived it. Paul names only one function. It is the forceful administration of vengeance — God's wrath — and justice. Nygren puts it thus: "The earthly ruler is *the servant of God in the aeon of wrath*. It is the instrument of God's wrath, and as such it bears the sword which, by the will of God, is to be used to combat evil."[61]

Through this function of the state the Christian benefits. The question now arises: How can Paul be correct with this statement that the application of the wrath of God by the most evil state can work to the benefit of the Christian? What Paul could not have meant is that the state in itself was good. He knew the Roman and Jewish authorities too well for that.[62] Neither could he have meant that the government would do the Christians direct good.[63] This must be said for the same reasons. He is speaking precisely of the good which the Christian derives from the retributive system of governmental authority. The good, of which he is speaking, must be the good of common morality which is inherent in all governmental order as opposed to anarchy.[64] The deduction can therefore be made that the most evil human government will produce the benefits Paul mentions here.

At this point one perhaps does best by letting a modern writer speak. Brunner has analyzed this aspect of good derived from the most evil systems of authority. Anarchy in the world is sinful, depraved beings must be checked at all costs. Anarchy, "the *bellum omnium contra omnes,*" in this sinful society is much worse than the worst state. This understanding makes the state a necessity.[65]

Of the evil state, and the good derived from it, Brunner goes on,

Even if that power is exercised by a despot devoid of any intention of justice, the mere fact that this central will exists, and effectively claims for itself the monopoly of coercive power, that above all, by claiming for itself the power over life and death, it removes that most dangerous element from the hands of the individual, has a beneficent influence. The state of anarchy ceases . . . a certain order of peace, however brutal, is established . . . The monopolization of power . . . though unintentionally, [has] this peaceable effect . . . [and] justice is . . . possible since the mutual use of force by individuals is eliminated . . . Even without wishing to, the unified coercive power safeguards the life of the individuals against each other by reserving to itself the right to kill . . .

Even the despot cannot rule in the long run without transforming the capricious dictates of his personal will into a generally valid law. . . . Even though this law springs from no intention of justice, but merely from the lust of power, it is, quite involuntarily, effective in the sense of justice.[66]

He goes on to show that this law will circumscribe partly the despot's own arbitrariness.[67]

In view of the universal application of Paul's teaching, and in view of what he evidently knew about evil in human government, it is this benefit which Paul means which will result from the application of the vengeance of God in sinful society by the agency of the state. It must also follow from this that there is always the possibility of greater benefit from a more just state.

That God bears a definite relationship to the state and its individual functionary is clear. It is also clear from the passage that it does not demand an interpretation which would ascribe divinity either to the state or the state's functionaries. Paul, however, lays down the principle that the state is God's arrangement and He uses it and its functionaries to accomplish part of His purpose.

It must, therefore, be concluded that this passage neither affirms nor denies the demonic element in state and state government. However, it seems to affirm the fact of the power of choice of the state and its rulers otherwise they would not possess what is meant by "power, authority" (*exousia*). Therefore, it can be further affirmed that there is no conflict in Paul's view of the state as given here and implied from other passages. Neither is there conflict with the view derived from the teachings of Jesus. But since from the teaching elsewhere the demonic element in the world government has been deduced, it must be accepted that, while Paul does not specifically mention it here, he assumes it as he presents facts from other angles.[68]

Bearing the threefold conclusion in mind that this passage teaches that the state and its representatives have the power of choice, that God is responsible for the arrangement of human government and has appointed it and its functionaries the task of dealing out his wrath upon evil, and by punishment procure and maintain a relative justice; and that Paul elsewhere plainly teaches a demonic element in human government which is not denied here, an effort of synthesis is in place.

When Paul wrote, Nero was the emperor of Rome. A more wicked ruler is difficult to imagine. But he was not yet, at the time of writing Romans, the matricide, the bloody tyrant, nor the persecutor of Christians.[69] However, one cannot possibly entertain the thought that the mere absence of some of the darker sins of Nero's career till the time of Paul's writing would have conditioned Paul's view. Apart from Paul's function as an inspired writer, he was too realistic a thinker and Christian for this. He must have known Herod. He was as evil as Nero.[70] His direct and bloody assault against God's purpose in the murderous attempt to kill the child Jesus[71] must have been fully known by Paul. There had been the bloody Sanhedrin which crucified Christ and allowed Stephen to be stoned. He knew Pilate, a full representative of the Roman government, and his inhuman act of delivering Jesus to be crucified. He must have remembered his own infamous career under the "powers that were" as he raised havoc with the church.[72] The Herod who slew James and who entertained evil intentions toward Peter was undoubtedly taken into account.[73] Further, one is reminded "that this exhortation was addressed to the Romans, when the cruelties and crimes of a Tiberius, Caligula, and Claudius were in yet fresh remembrance . . ."[74]

What Paul also knew with reference to these evil powers and men was that God somehow made them accomplish His purpose. They were the instruments of sin, but by God's guiding and restraining hand He accomplished His purpose without becoming implicated in their sin or curbing their power of choice.

"A striking case in point is Pharaoh, mentioned in 9, [verse] 17 of Romans, perhaps as hardened a ruler as ever lived; God himself indicates his great providential purpose in raising him to the throne."[75]

Paul's concept of the function of the state seems to be precisely what God had revealed about a number of heathen states in the Old Testament. The "Assyrian" was the "rod" of God's wrath. With him God accomplished the chastisement of Israel,[76] but in doing so, the king of Assyria incurred guilt. God asserts that He will punish the king.[77] Again, God says of Cyrus, king of the Medo-Persian empire, that he is "my shepherd, and shall perform all my pleasure . . ."[78] God calls Nebuchadnezzar "His servant" three times when He refers to the king's dealing with Israel.[79]

The clear fact is that these men and their states were simply tools in the hand of God to accomplish His purpose. The evil and sin perpetrated by these men and nations are not in point. It is rather the providential operation of God, without his own moral involvement, which caused them to accomplish His purpose.

In view of the solidarity of Scriptural teaching and the clear illustration of the teaching from the life and death of Jesus, plus Paul's own statements, one can conclude that Paul had in mind this type of God's providential dealing through governments, when he spoke of them as doing the service of God. This means that God uses the state as an instrument of His wrath irrespective of the intentions, morality, and wills of the rulers. This concept is supported by the fact that the immediate rulers which Paul must have had in mind knew nothing of the will of God, and, no doubt, would have cared less for it had they known it. Yet they are described by Paul as being God's agents.[80]

That this is the only possible view to take has been demonstrated by history. God cannot be involved in the crime of condemning Jesus, as has been shown. Neither can He be implicated in the crimes which have been directly inflicted on His children in the hideous persecutions which have marked the history of the church.[81] To impugn God for the sentencing of pure Christian virgins to the brothel,[82] by asserting the will of the magistrate to be the will of God is the height of incongruity. From this it must follow that all sin and injustice in history is not the act of God. The acts and voice of human government are not the acts and voice of God.[83]

There can be therefore no doubt about Paul's position. He was fully aware of the demonic in human government as evil men were "energized" by the prince of the power of the air,[84] and opposed God. He was also fully aware that God in His providence would bring about His ultimate purpose.[85] He knew that the sin which the state committed was not God's act, nor was the command of the state the command of God to the Christians.[86]

The discussion of this question can perhaps best be concluded with a statement from Lenski. After having considered the problem of evil and evil men in the state he says,

They change nothing regarding God's arrangement (*diatage*) of state authority. His institution of marriage stands, no matter what abuses men perpetrate. His institution of Christian congregations and of the Christian Church stands, despite what some congregations and some churches do. To imagine for one moment that God is involved when tyrants and popes arise is a misapprehension. God reckons with every one of them. No Nero can possibly alter the facts and the principles here laid down.[87]

The actual relations of the Christian to the state is the final question to be answered from Romans thirteen. The pivotal point of the Christian's relation to the state which Paul presents is submission to it. He says, "Let every soul be subject (*hupotassestho*) to the higher powers."[88] Thayer defines this word ". . . to subordinate; to subject, put in subjection . . . to obey . . ."[89] The present imperative form suggests individual, voluntary submission and forms a command. "Every soul" refers undoubtedly to every Christian. He is instructing Christians. It may have a wider reference but this cannot be maintained from the statement. The reason he gives is that human government is an arrangement of God.

The opposite of "being subject" (*hupotasso*), as used by Paul in giving the reason for submission to the authorities, is "to resist" (*antitasso*). This word is defined as ". . . to range in battle against; mid. to oppose one's self, resist."[90] This word denotes primarily violent resistance. This is the resistance which Paul forbids. It is the resistance against the authority. Then Paul asserts that this resister sets himself against (*anthistemi*) God's arrangement. This term means "to set against . . . resist, oppose . . ."[91] Since the form is perfect active indicative, Robertson defines it thus: "has taken his stand against."[92]

The crucial question which must be answered is: What does this obedience to the state mean? *Hupotasso* is used some forty times in the New Testament.[93] It is used of demons submitting to the command of expulsion.[94] It is used of the church's subjection to Christ.[95] It is also used of the wife's relationship to her husband,[96] of servants to their masters[97] and in many other similar ways. That the word means obedience is clear from its usage. However, there seems to be more in the word than obedience. Karl Barth, speaking of a case in which he thinks disobedience to the state is necessary, clarifies his stand thus:

> . . . even then the "subjection" will not cease. But their submission, their *respect* for the power of the State to which they continue to give what they owe, will consist in becoming its victim . . ."[98]

This answer presupposes the question of the degree of obedience which the Christian must render the state. There are only two alternatives. It must either be absolute or relative obedience. In view of what the state is, as shown from the New Testament and history, absolute obedience could not have been Paul's meaning.[99]

Having accepted the alternative that Paul must have meant relative and not absolute obedience, presents what seems to be another problem equally as crucial and difficult. What are the criteria by which the Christian can judge in what he can and must be obedient to the state? There seems to be only one answer. The Christian can do that which is morally right. He must refrain from what is morally wrong. There can be no other criterion. However, even this does not present the solution to the Christian. There is still the question whether an act when done as an individual Christian is sin but when a similar act is done as a representative of the state is not sinful. In other words, it is the problem of "private" and "official" ethics. Can the Christian do through, on behalf of, or under the state that which he cannot do as an individual without committing sin?

The whole body of New Testament revelation is specific on what for the Christian as an individual constitutes sin and what does not. However, the New Testament knows no other code of ethics than that for the individual Christian. If this is so, what happens when the view is accepted that the Christian can do under the state, or as a functionary of it, what he cannot do as an individual? If the New Testament gives no ethical standards or criteria with which to govern the Christian acting in an "official" capacity as contrasted with acting as an individual, from where can he derive the ethical code or principles which he must follow in his official conduct? The answer is that the Christian is left with principles and standards of ethics which cannot be tested by the New Testament and are thus the product of human philosophy and necessarily totally pragmatic. The precariousness of this position is obvious.

However, there seems to be in Scripture a strong indication that this duality of ethical standards does not exist. Karl Barth shows that in those passages of the epistles, which are directly concerned with the problem of the Christian and the state, the Christian is commanded to practice the same relations to all men as to the state. Barth writes,

The behaviour towards the State which they [the Scriptures] demand from all Christians is always connected with their behaviour towards *all* men. "Render therefore to *all* their dues . . . Owe *no man* anything but . . . to love one another (Rom xiii. 7, 8). In I Timothy ii. 1 we read that they should make "supplications, prayers, intercessions and giving of thanks for *all* men," Finally in I Peter ii. 13 we are again dealing with the "every ordinance of man," and later in v. 17, going a step further . . . "honour all men."[100]

Further, it must be noticed that one of Paul's arguments to support the injunction to obedience to the state is the Christian's conscience.[101] On this problem Riddle says, "When the civil power contradicts God's Word and His voice in our conscience, then it contradicts and subverts its own authority."[102] The conscience, to be accurate, is dependent upon the standard of ethics as presented by the teaching of Jesus and the apostles.[103]

There is also the conclusion which was drawn from the words of Jesus in which He stated and implied that Caiaphas, Pilate, and the soldiers incurred personal guilt in spite of the fact that they, for the most part, acted in governmental capacity and as its instruments.[104]

The necessary conclusions from these considerations seem to be that whatever the Scriptures do not permit the Christian to do in private relationships cannot be done by him at the dictates of the state. The implications of this conclusion are far-reaching.

Immediately preceding and succeeding Romans 13:1-7, Paul has given a number of clear injunctions about a Christian's conduct toward his fellow men.[105] A number of these injunctions are closely and concretely related to the question of a Christian's relation to the state, if the arguments here presented are valid. First, Paul forbids all revenge. This, as has been pointed out from the Sermon on the Mount, is actually the administration of justice.[106] God is going to take charge of all revenge. Then Paul goes on to exhort the Christian to do positive good to the enemy. All this is in harmony with Jesus' teaching of nonresistance and love.[107]

In the section following the passage on the state, Paul reiterates a number of items from the Mosaic moral law and adds the injunction of love. He shows that love will not do evil or injury.[108]

However emphatically the Christians are given these negative and positive injunctions, the retributional system of the state is dedicated to the very things which are forbidden to the Christian, because it is the instrument of the vengeance of God. This means that, what the Christian is forbidden, it is assumed that the state will find it necessary to do. Further, what the Christian is enjoined to do the state cannot do. A few brief quotations, dealing with the most basic elements of Christianity will point this up.

The late Archbishop Temple has spoken of the problem of the state and the Christian ethic. Hutchinson puts Temple's concept thus: ". . . there can be no forgiveness after the pattern of Christ on the cross . . . without self-immolation, and no nation is capable of that."[109] Again, Brunner says, "The state cannot be governed and ought not to be governed in accordance with the law of love . . ."[110]

If the premises in this line of argument are granted, one must concur with Dodd. Speaking of the state as an instrument of God's wrath and the Christian, referring to Romans chapters 12 and 13, he says,

> . . . the retributive system of justice in a non-Christian society is . . . a manifestation of the . . . principle (of wrath). The Christian order of society rests on a different and higher principle, which was expounded in chap. xii., and is succinctly stated in xiii. 8-10. The Christian takes no part in the administration of a retributive system; but, in so far as it serves moral ends, he must submit to it.[111]

This seems to have been the precise view of the early church.[112] Since the early church stood in close proximity of time and circumstance to the apostles, their view is of importance on the subject.

After Paul has given the injunction of obedience and submission he gives the reasons why the Christian must conform. The first reason is that to do otherwise than to submit is to resist. And resistance against the authorities and rulers is resistance (*anthistemi*) against the arrangement of God. To make this a valid reason for submission, it would seem that all *de facto* governments are implied. This would be in harmony with Peter's dictum of submitting to "every ordinance of man."[113]

There is a consequence attached to withstanding the arrangement of God. The consequence is damnation (*krima*), according to King James version. It is difficult to determine what Paul means by this term. There seem to be good reasons for Dodd's view. Taking the purpose of government into consideration as stated by Paul, Dodd suggests that it is the natural effect of the retributive system.[114] It is this type of cause and effect which Paul has spoken of as the wrath of God in Romans one.

Verse 3a gives another reason for submission. It is because the rulers are not a terror to good works but to evil. As has already been intimated, this statement must have reference to the common morality without which no society can exist with any measure of coherence. A minimum of this, as pointed out, exists under the worst rulers.

Verses 3b to four contain the warning to the Christian that he can have praise from the rulers only as he does the good. Otherwise he, too, will be subject to the consequences which must be meted out under the retributive system of the state.

But not only because of fearing retribution but for conscience sake the Christian must be subject.[115] It is not easy to determine what the standard is on which conscience is based. It seems that it is either that the Christian has recognized the moral value of the state, or because of the fact that the Christian is *commanded* to be subject to the state. The latter concept accords well with Peter's view which he expresses thus. "Be subject . . . for the Lord's sake."[116]

Verse six gives the reason for paying taxes. The way Paul makes the statement with "tribute" (*teleite,* present active indicative) makes the payment of tribute an assumption. The immediate reason for paying taxes is the Christian's conscience. It is not clear whether Paul includes fear of the rulers as a reason.[117] This, however, is likely.

Paul summarizes, in verse seven the general positive aspect of obedience and subjection. To give to all their due is the responsibility of the Christian. It is to be noted that Paul here uses the same word and form of the verb to enjoin the repayment of the Christian's due as Jesus used in His famous statement in Matt. 22:21. It is likely that this injunction was already universally accepted in the Christian community.

In the Pastoral Epistles.—There are two brief passages in the Pastoral Epistles which deal with the Christian and the state.[118]

The general chronological setting of the Pastorals has already been mentioned.[119] It remains only to examine the content of these passages.

I Timothy 2:1-4 is an exhortation to the Christian to pray for all men. Thanksgiving is to be included. The Greek synonyms for praying need not be examined separately. The three words suggest the different aspects of proper praying. After the general designation of the objects for prayer, Paul makes two specific references. The "kings" (*basileon*) and "all those in authority" (*panton ton en huperoche onton*) are kings and men in places of authority.[120] It is to be observed that *basileon* is plural. This makes the term comprehensive.[121]

This is clearly an exhortation to the Christian to fulfill a responsibility which he owes to the government. The responsibility is owed regardless of the type of ruler. This can be inferred from the general comprehensiveness of the exhortation.

Paul, however, gives what seem to be three other reasons for this prayer. First, this will benefit the Christians.[122] Second, it is the will of God.[123] Third, it is the desire of God that the ones prayed for will be saved.[124]

There is another inference which can be drawn. The prayer for kings and rulers presupposes the power of God to use them for His purpose.

The Titus passage[125] is more or less an abbreviation of Romans 13:1-7. It emphasizes subjection and obedience to rulers. Paul commands Titus to remind the Cretan Christians of these things.

It is not necessary to deal with what is essentially the same teaching Paul gave in Romans. However, there are in this passage significant additions to what Paul has said elsewhere. These must be briefly discussed.

It has been observed that Paul gave no qualifying statement to his command of submission to the state in Romans. In Titus, however, after he has exhorted to submission and obedience, he emphasizes the Christian's readiness to do every good work. This conditions the command to obedience. It is not absolute obedience which is enjoined. Rather, it is obedience which is active when good is to be done. What was assumed in Romans is here specifically stated.[126]

Neither were the Christians to speak evil of the rulers. They must not be contentious. Robertson characterizes the statement thus: "To be non-fighters."[127] They must be gentle, ". . . not pressing their own right, making allowances . . ."[128] They must display "perfect gentleness to all men."[129]

But these injunctions were to be carried out, not only to rulers, but toward all men. The language in this passage as also in like passages throughout the New Testament, seemingly, knows of no circumstances or conditions in which this non-resistance is not to be carried out.

Paul's Example

Its relation to the subject.—The view of inspiration assumed in this discussion does not include the inspiration of the acts

97

of the inspired writers. This means that these writers, while being guarded from all error in writing, were capable of errors in their personal lives.

Two examples show this clearly. On one occasion the great apostle Paul had a sharp contention with his missionary companion, Barnabas.[130] Peter also grievously deviated. Paul records that Peter was to be blamed for compromising the truth of the gospel by his actions.[131]

Consequently, in using the examples of the apostles as demonstrating the truth they taught, there enters a problem which was not present in the case of Jesus' example. The apostles can err in their acts. Jesus could not. This must be clearly borne in mind in the discussion.

Paul's example in Acts.—Paul at times clashed with the government authorities. Three of these occasions as recorded in Acts will be examined.[132]

The first is Paul's and Silas's flogging and imprisonment at Philippi and their release. Paul and Silas were Roman citizens. This meant that they were exempt from flogging. However, when they were taken at Philippi they were beaten and put in prison. The open prison and the attempted suicide of the warden and other elements in the narrative need not be discussed. The point is, that when Paul and Silas were sent word that they had been released, Paul did not accept this release privately. He asked for personal, and perhaps public, release from the magistrates themselves. He based his demand on the privilege which accrued to his Roman citizenship.

This act of Paul has been alleged as being a full assertion of his Roman citizenship.[133] The question arises: How does Paul's act accord with His teaching of nonresistance.

A brief analysis is in order. First, it is plain that Paul asks for a privilege from the magistrates on the basis of his citizenship. No reason is given for this action. Apparently the results of this action might have helped the local Christians in their relations with the authorities.[134] It might, however, have resulted in the exact opposite. Second, it must be remembered that Paul and Silas remained in prison at night when, it seems evident, they could have escaped. This means that they were submissive and obedient. Third, they, according to Roman law, could have asserted their full privilege by appealing for redress for the criminal treatment received. This would have meant direct action against, and obviously injury to, the magistrates who perpetrated the act.[135] This Paul did not do. He asked only for that privilege which involved no coercion, resistance, or injury to another person. If he asserted his full privilege of citizenship he would have been involved in doing these very things.

On another occasion Paul appealed to Caesar for his trial.[136] Paul had been rescued from mob violence by the Romans.[137] He was standing trial. The Jews were present to accuse Paul. Paul made his defense. Finally Festus asks whether Paul would go to Jerusalem to be tried by the Sanhedrin. This Paul did not permit. He says that he has done no wrong to the Jews and refuses to be given back to the Jews. It seems that the only way to block this move is to invoke his citizen privilege and appeal to the highest tribunal. He appealed to Caesar.

A few salient points must be examined. First, the privilege which Paul invoked could not result in any injury to anyone concerned. There was no litigation against any man or party. Second, it must be noticed that no verdict had yet been pronounced. Third, it was a mere matter of choice between two tribunals—one, which in his case had all the evidence of being a mob affair and one which perhaps would give Paul his liberty. Fourth, it is even possible that Paul remembered the revelation that he was yet to go to Rome.[138] This might have motivated him in his decision.

With these considerations in mind it can be concluded that these occasions reveal nothing in the conduct of Paul which is contrary to his teaching on the Christian's relation to the state. Nor does his action contradict the doctrine of non-resistance as has been discussed.

The third occasion[139] to be examined falls into a different category. Paul is before the Sanhedrin. During the court procedure, Ananias, the high priest, commanded the ones who stood near to Paul to smite him. This evidently provoked Paul. He uses strong language against the high priest. However "he does not imprecate vengeance on him."[140]

Regardless of the exact nature of Paul's provocation, he admits error. It is therefore not possible to relate this incident to his teaching.

FOOTNOTES

[1]Anders Nygren, *Commentary on Romans,* trans. Carl C. Rasmussen (Philadelphia: Muhlenberg Press, 1949), p. 429.

[2]I Cor. 6:12a.

[3]I Cor. 6:9, 10.

[4]I Cor. 7:17-24.

[5]Gavin, *op. cit.,* p. 9.

[6]Holmes Rolston, *The Social Message of the Apostle Paul* (Richmond: John Knox Press, 1942), pp. 195 ff.

[7]Cf. Lee, *op. cit.,* p. 75.

[8]*Vide supra,* pp. 56f; cf. *supra* pp. 35 ff.

[9]Rom. 1; Eph. 2:1, 2.

[10]Eph. 6:12.

[11]II Cor. 4:4.

[12]Oscar Cullmann, *Christ and Time,* trans. Floyd V. Filson (London: S C M Press, Ltd., 1951), p. 191.

[13]Henry Clarence Thiessen, *Introduction to the New Testament* (Grand Rapids: Wm. B. Eerdmans Publishing Company, 1943), pp. 263, 266, 269. Cf. Schaff, *op. cit.,* I, 378.

[14]II Tim. 4:6-8.

[15]I Tim. 2:1-4; Tit. 3:1, 2.

[16]William Sanday and Arthur C. Headlam, *A Critical and Exegetical Commentary on the Epistle to the Romans* ("The International Critical Commentary"; New York: Charles Scribner's Sons, 1895), p. 371.

[17]J. P. Lange and F. R. Fay, *Epistle of Paul to the Romans*, trans. J. F. Hurst; rev. and ed. P. Schaff and M. B. Riddle ("A Commentary on the Holy Scriptures"; New York: Charles Scribner's Sons, 1892), p. 398.

[18]Merrill C. Tenney, *The New Testament: an Historical and Analytic Survey* (Grand Rapids: Wm. B. Eerdmans Publishing Company, 1953), pp. 359 ff.

[19]I Pet. 2:13-25.

[20]Cf. Tenney, *op. cit.*, p. 359.

[21]Alvah Hovey, (ed.), *Commentary on the Epistle to the Romans* ("An American Commentary on the New Testament"; Philadelphia: American Baptist Publication Society, 1886), p. 117.

[22]F. Godet, *Commentary on St. Paul's Epistle to the Romans*, trans. A. Cusin (New York: Funk & Wagnalls, Publishers, 1883), p. 440.

[23]Nygren, *op. cit.*, p. 426.

[24]*Ibid.*

[25]Sanday and Headlam, *op. cit.*, p. 366.

[26]Cf. Rom. 12:9-21 with 13:8, 9.

[27]Rom. 12:3-8.

[28]Rom. 12:9-21.

[29]Rom. 13:1-7.

[30]Nygren, *op. cit.*, p. 429.

[31]"*exousia*," *A Greek-English Lexicon of the New Testament.*

[32]*Ibid.*

[33]John 19:10, 11.

[34]Cf. Rom. 13:3-6.

[35]Matt. 22:21. *Vide supra*, pp. 48 ff.

[36]Cf. R. C. H. Lenski, *The Interpretation of St. Paul's Epistle to the Romans* (Columbus: Lutheran Book Concern, 1936), pp. 788 ff.

[37]William G. T. Shedd, *A Critical and Doctrinal Commentary Upon the Epistle of St. Paul to the Romans* (New York: Charles Scribner's Sons, 1879), p. 377. Cf. Sanday and Headlam, *op. cit.*, p. 366.

[38]Lange and Fay, *Epistle of Paul to the Romans*, p. 398.

[39]Robertson, *Word Pictures in the New Testament*, IV, 407.

[40]Cf. "*apo*" and "*hupo*," "*A Greek-English Lexicon of the New Testament.*

[41]Behm, "*exousia*," "*Theologisches Woerterbuch zum Neuen Testament*, Vol. II.

[42]Matt. 28:18.

[43]Cf. Strack and Billerbeck, *op. cit.*, III, 303.

[44]Cf. C. H. Dodd, *The Epistle of Paul to the Romans* ("The Moffatt New Testament Commentary"; New York: Harper and Brothers, Publishers, 1932), p. 203.

[45]"*diatage*," *A Greek-English Lexicon of the New Testament.*

[46]"tasso," Ibid.

[47]"tasso," Henry George Liddell and Robert Scott, A Greek-English Lexicon, (rev. ed.; Oxford: At the Clarendon Press, n.d.).

[48]Cf. "tasso," The Englishman's Greek Concordance of the New Testament.

[49]Cf. Lenski, op. cit., p. 792.

[50]Ibid., p. 797.

[51]Rom. 13:3.

[52]Rom. 13:4.

[53]Rom. 13:6.

[54]Cf. Sanday and Headlam, op. cit., p. 367.

[55]Robertson, Word Pictures in the New Testament, IV, 407.

[56]Sanday and Headlam, op. cit., p. 367.

[57]Lenski, op. cit., p. 795.

[58]Robertson, Word Pictures in the New Testament, IV, 408.

[59]Lenski, op. cit., p. 800.

[60]Godet, op. cit., p. 445.

[61]Nygren, op. cit., p. 429.

[62]Cf. Lenski, op. cit., p. 797.

[63]Ibid.

[64]Cf. Dodd., op. cit., p. 203.

[65]Brunner, Justice and the Social Order, p. 197.

[66]Ibid., pp. 197 f.

[67]Ibid.

[68]On the treatment of the demonic element in human government, vide supra, pp. 38 ff.; 56 ff.; 63 ff.

[69]Lenski, op. cit., p. 797.

[70]Ibid.

[71]Matt. 2:16, 18.

[72]Acts 8:1-3.

[73]Acts 12:1-3.

[74]Lange and Fay, Epistle of Paul to the Romans, p. 398.

[75]Lenski, op. cit., p. 792.

[76]Isa. 10:5-12.

[77]Isa. 10:13 ff.

[78]Isa. 44:28.

[79]Jer. 25:9; 27:6; 43:10.

[80]Rom. 13:1-7.

[81]Herbert Brook Workman, Persecutions in the Early Church (London: C. H. Kelly, 1906), passim.

[82]Ibid., pp. 288 ff.

[83]Cf. Dodd, op. cit., p. 203; cf. Lange and Fay, Epistle of Paul to the Romans, p. 398.

[84]Eph. 2:2.

[85]Cf. Rom. 9:16 ff.

[86]Cf. Dodd., *op. cit.,* p. 203.

[87]Lenski, *op. cit.,* p. 797.

[88]Rom. 13:1.

[89]"*hupotasso,*" *A Greek-English Lexicon of the New Testament.*

[90]"*antitasso,*" *Ibid.*

[91]"*anthistemi,*" *Ibid.*

[92]Robertson, *Word Pictures in the New Testament,* IV, 407.

[93]Cf. "*hupotasso,*" *The Englishman's Greek Concordance of the New Testament,*

[94]Luke 10:17, 20.

[95]Eph. 5:24.

[96]Eph. 5:22.

[97]Tit. 2:9.

[98]Karl Barth, *Church and State,* trans. G. Ronald Howe (London: Student Christian Movement Press, 1939), p. 68.

[99]Dodd, *op. cit.,* p. 203; Godet, *op. cit.,* p. 442; Robertson, *Word Pictures of the New Testament,* IV, 407; Lange and Fay, *Epistle of Paul to the Romans,* p. 398; Acts 4:19, 5:29; Loraine Boettner, *The Christian Attitude Toward War* (2d ed., rev.; Grand Rapids: Wm. B. Eerdmans Publishing Co., 1942), p. 40; Barth, *op. cit.,* pp. 64 f.; Tit. 3:1.

[100]Barth, *op. cit.,* p. 48.

[101]Rom. 13:5.

[102]Lange and Fay, *Epistle of Paul to the Romans,* p. 398.

[103]O. Hallesby, *Conscience,* trans. Clarence J. Carlsen (7th ed.; Minneapolis: Augsburg Publishing House, 1938), p. 141.

[104]*Vide supra,* pp. 65 f.

[105]Rom. 12:17-21; 13:8-10.

[106]Cf. Lenski, *op. cit.,* pp. 797 f.

[107]Cf. Dodd, *op. cit.,* p. 200, also Matt. 5:38-48.

[108]Rom. 13:10. Cf. "*kakos,*" *A Greek-English Lexicon of the New Testament.*

[109]Hutchinson, *op. cit.,* p. 164.

[110]Brunner, *The Divine Imperative,* p. 462.

[111]Dodd, *op. cit.,* p. 204.

[112]*Vide supra,* pp. 23 ff.

[113]I Pet. 2:13.

[114]Cf. Dodd, *op. cit.,* p. 204.

[115]Rom. 13:5.

[116]I Pet. 2:13.

[117]Cf. Sanday and Headlam, *op. cit.,* p. 368.

[118]I Tim. 2:1-4; Tit. 3:1-3.

119*Vide supra*, pp. 77 f.

120E. F. Scott, *The Pastoral Epistles* ("The Moffat New Testament Commentary"; London: Hodder and Stoughton, 1948), p. 19.

121*Ibid.*, W. M. Ramsay, *The Church in the Roman Empire* (London: G. P. Putnam's Sons, 1911), p. 250.

122I Tim. 2:2b.

123I Tim. 2:3.

124I Tim. 2:4.

125Tit. 3:1, 2.

126Rom. 13:1.

127Robertson, *Word Pictures in the New Testament*, IV, 606.

128Alvah Hovey (ed.) *Commentary on the Pastoral Epistles* ("An American Commentary on the New Testament"; Philadelphia: American Baptist Publication Society, 1886), p. 141.

129Scott, *The Pastoral Epistles*, p. 72.

130Acts 15:39.

131Gal. 2:11-21.

132Acts 16:36-39; 25:10-12; 23:1-5.

133R. C. H. Lenski, *The Interpretation of the Acts of the Apostles* (Columbus: Lutheran Book Concern, 1934), p. 682.

134F. F. Bruce, *The Acts of the Apostles* (2d ed., London: The Tyndale Press, 1952), p. 323.

135George H. Allen, "Roman Law," *The International Standard Bible Encyclopedia*, IV, 2611 ff.

136Acts 25:10-12.

137Acts 21:27-36.

138Acts 23:11.

139Acts 23:1-5.

140Alvah Hovey (ed.), *Commentary on the Acts of the Apostles*, ("An American Commentary on the New Testament"; Philadelphia: American Baptist Publication Society, 1886), p. 263.

CHAPTER V

PETER AND THE CHRISTIAN'S RELATION TO THE STATE

Peter's Teaching

General considerations.—The final passage of Scripture which deals specifically with the problem of the Christian's relation to the state is found in Peter's writings.[1]

Peter's agreement with Paul on this subject is remarkable. The agreement is so great that the view has often been taken that a borrowing one from the other must have occurred. Selwyn, however, suggests that "A common source underlying all the passages is more probable . . ."[2]

The date of the composition of the epistle is important. If Thiessen can be followed, the letter was written approximately 65 A.D.[3] This would mean that the Neronian persecution had already started.[4] It is not possible to obtain evidence that this persecution spread to the provinces. It is, however, possible that it did. There is the strong probability that the provinces were influenced by the example set at Rome. As a consequence it is to be expected that persecution would break out in those localities where hatred for Christians ran high.[5] This could well have been the case in Asia Minor. It is to the Christians of these areas that Peter addresses this first letter.

While it is not clear whether these Christians in Asia Minor were already caught in a persecution at the time of the writing of the letter or whether there was anticipation that it would come, one thing is certain: Peter's letter abounds with advice to the Christians on how to honor Christ in the severest trials and sufferings.[6]

The apostle Peter takes a number of different human relationships into consideration[7] in his exhortation to the Christian. In each of these relations, the basic element which is to characterize the Christian's attitude and action is subjection, submission. It is to be observed that both personal and civic relations are included. He refers to the relations of the Christian to civil government and of the household slave to his master.[8] Having given his intended exhortation, he uses the conduct of Jesus in his trial and crucifixion as the example which the Christians are to follow.

The introduction of Jesus' conduct as an example raises a question of context. Is the example of Jesus meant to be related to more of the context than only to the instruction of slaves? It is to be observed that the passage about Christ's example follows immediately after the exhortations to the servants. However, the view taken in this examination is that the example of Jesus was meant to be related to the teaching of the Christian and civil government as much as to the other passages. There are three valid reasons for this view.

First, in both passages the same word for subjection is used. This points to the similarity of the subjection. Second, in some respects the example of Jesus is more closely related to the teaching on subjection to the civil authorities because that was specifically what Jesus exemplified. Third, it is to be observed that the apostle commences[9] with a broad topical sentence when he commands the Christians to be subject to "every ordinance of man." This statement plainly includes the human "ordinances" of slavery.[10]

106

It is therefore concluded that the example of Jesus as used by Peter was meant to be applied and followed in the Christian's obedience to the civil powers.

Exposition of I Peter 2:13-17.—To arrive at the meaning of this passage, four questions may be asked. First, of what civil government did the apostle Peter speak? Second, what was Peter's concept of the origin and nature of civil governments? Third, what is the function of human government? And fourth, how ought the Christian to be related to the state as it is expressed in human government?

If the given date of Peter's first epistle is correct, then it follows that Nero has already revealed his true character. From the Christian standpoint there perhaps could exist no more evil character or administration. Yet Peter specifically calls upon the Christians to submit themselves to the "king" as supreme. The term "king" is the regular Greek title for Caesar.[11] If Christians are called upon to be obedient and subject themselves to an evil man like Nero as civil ruler, it seems to follow that there can be no supreme ruler whom Christians are not obliged to obey. It must be remembered that both Paul and Peter use the same word — *hupotasso* — for obedience and subjection to rulers.

This factor and all that has been said on this point in relation to Paul's teaching makes it plain that Peter, as Paul, is laying down enduring principles which are meant to be valid throughout this age. It is plain that the character of the ruler does not invalidate the principle. The submission will always be the same. Active obedience will vary with the moral nature of the ruler's demands.[12]

In this brief statement, Peter reveals some aspects of his concept of civil government. He introduces the section with *anthropine ktisei* (human ordinance). The latter word can be defined as "the act of creation," " 'creation' in the concrete sense . . . 'a creature.' "[13] The former word, an adjective, gives the character to "creation" or institution. There is also the idea of origin. Of this expression, Selwyn says that it means a

. . . *fundamental social institution,* i.e., the State, household, and the family. *Ktisis* was the regular Greek term for the founding of a city . . . and it is in this sense rather than the usual O.T. sense of a divine creation that it is employed here: Though the idea that such an institution was part of God's plan for human life . . . was not excluded.[14]

There is no clash here with Paul's concept. Paul emphasized God's relation to human government in its source of authority and God's arrangement and use of government. This Peter does not contradict.[15] Peter, on the other hand, looks at the actual constitution of human government with its human origin and character. This, as has been seen, Paul does not contradict; he assumes it.

The state, as an institution, slavery[16] and marriage[17] are all subsumed under the designation of human institutions.[18] This concept accords well with the total teaching of Scripture. And the facts of history assume their proper dimensions under this concept.

On the function of the state, Paul and Peter agree again. The governors are sent by the king for vengeance on evil-doers. In Paul, however, the ruler who punishes for evil is God's instrument. In Peter, the immediate human agency is shown, although Robertson suggests that *di' autou* "is 'by God,' as Jesus made plain to Pilate; even Pilate received his authority ultimately 'from above' (John 18:11)."[19] Depending on the point of view, both concepts are correct.[20]

The second aspect of this function is spoken of as the praise of those doing well. The meaning of this clause is perhaps best shown by Hort. He writes,

Obviously the bestowal of praise is not one of the usual functions of magistrates, though public spirit, especially as shewn in munificence, was often celebrated in laudatory inscriptions which might often have originated with magistrates. But this kind of praise suits St. Paul's tone very ill, and his last cited clause (*theou gar k.t.l.*) points rather to such a praise as would at least not be discordant with the praise bestowed by God . . . The praise spoken of was a result of the civil government, not that it was in any sense pronounced by the civil government. The human justice administered by the magistrate and the holy life of the Christian, however far apart they might seem to be, had alike *to agathon* [the good] as their goal. The sense of right and wrong which the public administration of justice kept alive, was a powerful . . . factor . . .[21]

This points to the conclusion which was drawn from Paul's treatment of the same subject. The necessary justice under every state has a common area of morality with Christian ethics. To be sure, the purpose behind the demand for this morality is not identical, but it is present nonetheless. It is to be concluded that the absence of punishment, in effect, constitutes the praise.

The final question is that of the Christian's relation to civil government. Again, the basic aspect of this relation is "subjection" (*hupotasso*). It is obedience and subjection.[22] The verb is in the aorist imperative form. This subjection must characterize the Christian both in his relations to the king, or Caesar, and to those subordinates who are sanctioned by him. Paul has used the plural of king, as has been seen.[23] This included the Herods as sub-kings. That Peter also could not have meant absolute obedience is fully obvious.[24] However, a quotation from N. W. Williams is to the point. He says:

It was not necessary for Peter's purpose to remind them [the Christians] of the possible existence of such civil requirements as it would be sinful to obey . . . If by submitting to every ordinance of man he meant submitting even if it involved commission of sin, why did he not save himself from martyrdom?[25]

Peter goes on to give two reasons for this obedience and subjection to civil government. First he says, "for the Lord's sake" (*dia ton kurion*). Evidently, this phrase is closely related to Paul's concept of conscience.[26] Bigg points out that submission is for the Lord's sake ". . . because the Lord's life was one of obedience, because he Himself showed respect to Pilate, and because He commanded His people to obey. Matt. xxii. 21."[27]

The second reason Peter gives is that Christians should be subject and obedient to the rulers so that they would not give occasion for slander and evil report. This was not mentioned by Paul. It is possible that court trials are anticipated.[28]

In verse sixteen, Peter finally characterizes the submission of the Christian to civil authorities. Lenski suggests the meaning thus: "We subject ourselves to government for the Lord's sake as being perfectly free, in no way as slaves to men, how free Acts 4:19 and 4:29 indicate."[29] The absolute and perfect subjection is to God—"slaves of God" (*theou douloi*), but this freedom and this servanthood give no room for wickedness.[30]

Peter mentions only one specific element which must be done to the rulers. The Christians were to honor the king. This statement is conditioned by the expression "honour all men" (*pantas timesate*). By obedience this honor is rendered.[31]

There are three more elements which must be presented to gain a fuller meaning from the passage already considered. First, since Peter makes the subjection and obedience of the Christian an injunction with respect to "every ordinance of man," which includes civil government and slavery, the following verses, dealing with slavery and the slaves' relation to his master, must be considered.

It must be noticed that "subjection, obedience" (*hupotasso*) is here also used for the slave's relation to his master. The subjection and obedience of the slave is to be practiced in spite of the possibility of the severest of suffering.[32] The injunction becomes the more barbed by Peter's statement that no difference must be made between the good and "froward" master. The Christian must suffer patiently.[33] When the treatment of slaves and the circumstances of slavery of New Testament times are considered, the injunctions of Peter clearly prescribe the practice of nonresistance. There is no doubt that occasions arose when personal self-defense against evil masters was a possibility. But Peter enjoins submission. This nonresistance was to be exercised for conscience sake. Evidently resistance was considered sinful.[34]

Second, there is Peter's introduction of Christ in his trial and crucifixion as the supreme example of nonresistance for the Christian. As Christ did not resist but submitted when men did the worst to Him, so must the slave not resist but submit, even to the evil master.

The unity of the whole First Peter's passage under consideration demands that this example of Christ must also be applied to the Christian's relation to the state. Whatever the state does to the Christian, it is still the obligation of the Christian to submit and be obedient.

Third, there was the general persecution which was in the mind of the apostle Peter as he wrote.[35] It is significant to note that the early persecution had both an official and a private character. Government officials, soldiers, and private enemies were engaged in the persecutions. Professional extortioners wrung money from Christians by threats.[36] In all of these circumstances, the Christian was to be nonresistant. Christ's example, as used by Peter, is also applied to the Christian's conduct under the stress of persecution.[37]

It must be concluded from the above examination that in all the relation of the Christian to others, including the relation to the state, which the apostle Peter mentions, the Christian is to be totally nonresistant. The agreement of Peter with Paul and the teaching of Jesus makes the argument in favor of non-resistance conclusive.

Peter's Example

Twice in the Acts of the Apostles, the apostle Peter makes significant statements regarding his relation to the "powers that be."[38] When the Sanhedrin forbade the preaching of the gospel, Peter announced boldly in essence that to cease preaching would be disobedience to God. Thus, to be obedient to the "powers that be" (on the occasion) meant to be disobedient to God. This Peter could not do. His conclusion is: "We must obey God rather than men."[39]

There is one conclusion which can be drawn from the example of Peter. When he spoke of the Christian's obedience and submission to the state, he conditioned his injunctions by the will of God. The Christian's obedience to the state ceases where the disobedience to God begins.

FOOTNOTES

[1]I Pet. 2.13-25.

[2]Edward Gordon Selwyn, *The First Epistle of Peter* (London: Macmillan & Co., Ltd., 1947), p. 429.

[3]Thiessen, *op. cit.*, p. 285.

[4]Schaff, *op. cit.*, I, 378.

[5]*Ibid.*

[6]Cf. Tenney, *op. cit.*, p. 362.

[7]Cf. I Pet. 2:13-18; 3:1, 7.

[8]Robertson, *Word Pictures in the New Testament*, VI, 102.

[9]I Pet. 3:13.

[10]C. E. B. Cranfield, *The First Epistle of Peter* (London: S C M Press, Ltd., 1950), p. 57.

[11]Charles Bigg, *A Critical and Exegetical Commentary on the Epistles of St. Peter and St. Jude* ("The International Critical Commentary"; London: T. & T. Clark, 1901), p. 139.

[12]Cf. Cranfield, *op. cit.*, pp. 58 ff; Acts 4:19; 5:29.

[13]Bigg, *A Critical and Exegetical Commentary on the Epistles of St. Peter, St. John, and St. Jude*, p. 139.

[14]Selwyn, *op. cit.*, p. 172.

[15]R. C. H. Lenski, *The Interpretation of the Epistles of St. Peter, St. John, and St. Jude* (Columbus: Lutheran Book Concern, 1938), pp. 111 f.

[16]I Pet. 2:18.

[17]I Pet. 3:1.

[18]Cf. Nicoll, *op. cit.*, V, 59.

[19]Robertson, *Word Pictures in the New Testament*, VI, 101.

[20]Alvah Hovey (ed.), *Commentary on the Epistles of Peter* ("An American Commentary on the New Testament"; Philadelphia: American Baptist Publication Society, 1886), p. 32.

[21]F. J. A. Hort, *The First Epistle of St. Peter* I. 1-11, 17. (London: Macmillan and Co., Ltd., 1898), p. 142.

[22]Cf. *infra*, p. 138.

[23]I Tim. 2:2.

[24]Hovey, *Commentary on the Epistles of Peter*, VI, 31 ff.

[25]Cf. Cranfield, *op. cit.*, p. 59.

[26]*Vide supra*, p. 119.

[27]Bigg, *A Critical and Exegetical Commentary on the Epistles of St. Peter, St. John, and St. Jude*, p. 139.

[28]Cf. Nicoll, *op. cit.*, V, 60.

[29]Lenski, *The Interpretation of the Epistles of St. Peter, St. John and St. Jude*, p. 114.

[30]Cf. Selwyn, *op. cit.*, p. 174.

[31]James Moffat, *The General Epistles* ("The Moffat New Testament Commentary"; New York: Harper and Brothers Publishers, n.d.), p. 124.

[32]Cf. I Pet. 2:19, 20.

[33]I Pet. 2:20.

[34]Cf. I Pet. 2:19-22.

[35]Cf. I Pet. 3:8-18.

[36]Workman, *op. cit.*, p. 287; cf. *ibid.*, p. 98.

[37]Cf. I Pet. 3:8-21; 2:22-24.

[38]Acts 4:19; 5:29.

[39]Acts 5:29.

CHAPTER VI

JOHN AND THE CHRISTIAN'S RELATION TO THE STATE

His Teaching

In his first epistle.—The significant contributions which the apostle John makes in his first letter have already been pointed out. A summary statement is in order. What John emphasizes strongly is Satan's relation to unregenerate men.[1] In the final chapter of this epistle he sums up this aspect of his teaching by stating that ". . . the whole world lieth in the evil one."[2] The concept of the "world" (*kosmos*) must here be related to the problem of the book.

In the Apocalypse.—A thorough examination of all the material in the Apocalypse which seems relevant to the subject is not possible within the scope and the purpose of this book. It is also questionable whether its inclusion would be desirable because of the unique exegetical problems which are necessarily involved. Further, the diversity of opinions about the exegesis and meaning of the book which have been held by scholars, often of equal integrity and unquestioned motives, causes one to tread cautiously with reference to the Apocalypse. While recognizing these facts it is still possible to make some specific and general observations from this writing of the apostle John which will not violate the assumptions which have been made, nor contradict the exegesis of the most accepted major types of its interpretations.

The first consideration in the Apocalypse—the letter to the church at Pergamos[3]—is not subject to the problems of exegesis which have been mentioned above. This is evident from the fact that all four schools of interpretation which are currently generally accepted by one or the other of the exegetes of the book are agreed that the messages of John to the seven churches of Asia Minor are fully historical.[4] The apocalyptic and predictive elements enter only when figurative interpretations are superimposed on the facts of history as recorded.

A casual reading of this letter does not reveal any immediate and strong relevance to the problem of the Christian and the state, but when the historical bases for the statements in this message are examined, their applicability is obvious. Pergamos was the official capital of the Province and the seat of the Roman administration. Since Pergamos was the seat of the administrative capital, it was also the chief seat of the state religion. When the seven letters were written, ". . . the imperial government had already ranged itself definitely in opposition to the Church of Christ."[5] Ramsay goes on to show that "The procedure against the Christians was fixed and stereotyped. Their loyalty was now tested by the one criterion recognized alike by public opinion and by government policy, viz., their willingness to perform the ritual of the state religion . . ." which included Caesar worship.[6]

In view of these facts, Ramsay concludes that John only could have written to the church at Pergamos that they were dwelling where Satan's throne was and where Satan dwelt. If Ramsay's line of argumentation is accepted, it is the Roman state which is conceived of as being controlled by Satan and the arch-enemy of the church.

When one turns to the apocalyptic parts of Revelation, it is observed that the apostle clearly postulates the proposition that the government or governments which he describes are totally under demon control and fall under the judgment of

God.[7] These deductions from the Apocalypse alone cannot be considered conclusive that all human government, as revealed in John's visions and as evinced by contemporary Rome, has reached a high pitch of anti-Christian fury. If only the Apocalypse would have suggested this view of the demonic in human government, it could perhaps be concluded that John saw Satan's power revealed in the state only because of the magnitude of its opposition to the saints and their Christ. But now his conclusions are not surprising for both the undertone of the teaching of Jesus and Paul and their specific pronouncements have already revealed the basic concept, but it remained for John to give it more dominant and dramatic portrayal in the Apocalypse. It is, however, not too much to say that the total argument has gained cogency by the evidence from the last book of the Bible.

There are a few general observations which can also be made. In spite of the raging opposition of the state against the Christians, evidently resulting in much bloodshed, the saints are pictured as resting their case with God. They are patiently waiting for the vengeance and righteous wrath of God.[8] While the conditions underlying these revelations may be quite different from those in the Gospels or the Epistles, yet it is remarkable that the sentiment and the views are the same. The saints are also portrayed as those who disobey the dictates of the state when its commands abrogate the commandments of God even though their lives are endangered by this disobedience.[9]

Conclusion

In conclusion it can be said that Revelation breathes the air of complete separation between the Christian and the state. The reason is not far to seek. The Christian, the saint, is in the order of grace and the church is the bride of Jesus Christ. The state, as here pictured, is of the order of the "world" (*kosmos*)—human society outside of the order of grace, and standing in diametric opposition to God and Christ. This view of human society as outside of Christ and in opposition against Christ is essentially the concept of Jesus, John, and Paul. The concept finds its concrete expression in the moral meaning of the term "world." It is the practical demonstration of the moral distance between this society and God and His children, and its antagonism against them which is more fully expressed in the Apocalypse than in any previous writing in the New Testament.

FOOTNOTES

[1]John 3:8-12.
[2]I John 5:19.
[3]Rev. 2:12-17.
[4]Tenney, *op. cit.*, p. 407.
[5]W. M. Ramsay, *The Letters to the Seven Churches of Asia* (New York: A. C. Armstrong & Son, 1905), pp. 293 ff.
[6]*Ibid.*
[7]Rev. 13; 17; 19.
[8]Rev. 6:11; 17:6; 18:24.
[9]Cf. Rev. 13:17; 14:9-12.

CHAPTER VII

CONCLUSION

The New Testament clearly does not have as its purpose to give detailed information on the subject of the origin, nature, and function of the state and its government. In spite of this there is much material on these subjects in the Scriptures as they relate to the Christian and his moral conduct. This has been examined and a number of significant conclusions can be drawn from the results of this inquiry.

It has been found that it is impossible for the state to love as the New Testament commands the Christian to love, for the application of vengeance or justice is incompatible with this love and the forgiveness which is a necessary result of true love. But not to love and not to forgive is to sin. It has also been found in this examination that the state is obliged to do that which is forbidden to the Christian. Further, it has been shown that the state is a necessity in sinful society. It must therefore be concluded that the state exists as a *sinful necessity*. Therefore the state cannot be Christian.

This leads to another conclusion. The state is of the order of the "world" (*kosmos*) and therefore not of the order of grace. It is of that system which in some real and present way is controlled by Satan. Peter's concept of the state as a "human institution", having its origin in man and having human character points in the same direction. Human depravity is here assumed.

With the foregoing conclusions in mind and recognizing the necessary nature of the application of vengeance or justice, it can be maintained that the ultimate human basis of the existence of the state is the power of coercion. These facts lead to the further observation that the state must be dedicated to police action and at least some wars.

The function of the state is to apply God's wrath, which is described as the exercising of vengeance against evil. This has been shown to be the administration of justice which at its best can only be relative. From this function of human government the Christian benefits. The Christian, as one who does not commit "evil," will find praise from the "powers that be."

The state is God's arrangement and is appointed by him for the purpose of enforcing order and justice. The authority which the state and its functionaries exercise is not supreme, but is given of God. It secures the power of judicial choice itself but gives no indication of the morality or the immorality of the choice. It can further be concluded, therefore, that the *individuals* exercising the powers of state are responsible to God for the decisions they make.

The state, as God's arrangement and tool to accomplish His purpose, is not divine. Whatever is intended by the statement that the state is appointed by God and a servant in His hand, it cannot mean that God's moral character is in any way imprinted on the state. This is obvious from the conclusions which have already been drawn.

Further, it must be concluded that every *de facto* state is a *bona fide* state according to the New Testament. The Scriptures, moreover, assume the existence of the secular state till the end of the age. They also assume that Christians will live under this state.

For the Christian the New Testament clearly teaches subjection and obedience to the state. These are to be exercised in spite of the severe suffering which might be involved. Since, however, the state has the functions which involve sin, it is to be expected that the New Testament would teach a qualified obedience to the state. The subjection, however, must be total. This is precisely what it teaches when the total New Testament ethic is examined. And since the New Testament knows of only one ethic, the "personal" and "private" ethic, it is this which must be determinative of all the Christian's acts, whether of a private or of an official nature. Each moral act which the Christian perpetrates is totally his own responsibility. The Christian must do only right; he cannot permit any power to force him to sin.

Another significant deduction which must be made from this examination is that the New Testament teaches total nonresistance. All coercion is forbidden, which necessarily includes homicide. This nonresistance sets aside all pragmatic considerations and acts solely on the precepts of the New Testament. It permits, however, the use of petition, persuasion, and command, if morally right. It does not demand subjection to evil and injury when legitimate physical escape is morally possible. These conclusions lead to the further observations, when the Christian's total experience is considered, that this nonresistance must characterize his whole life. This nonresistant life includes attitudes and actions toward state authorities. It governs all private relationships. The same nonresistant relationship must exist between the Christian and foreign people and the foreign state for two reasons. One is that the basic meaning of nonresistance will not admit of any other relationship and the other is that Paul taught that every *de facto* government is a *bona fide* government, therefore subjection to the foreign state is also enjoined where the authority of that government over the Christian is fact.

From this study and the conclusions which have been made, it follows that the Christian cannot participate in any function of human government, or act on behalf of any state or society, which involves him in those things which God has forbidden the Christian. This means, specifically, that the Christian cannot participate in any function which is directly connected with the retributive action of the state. This conclusion no doubt, is far reaching. Niebuhr concludes that all politics are inconsistent with the nonresistant position. Of the one who takes the pacifist position he says, ". . . I for one will accord him my genuine respect and admiration if he leave the world of politics alone entirely and seek simply to live by the love commandment . . ."[1]

It has been concluded that the state is of the order of the "world" (*kosmos*). This leads to another conclusion with reference to the separation of the Christian from the state. If it is granted that the state is included in what the Bible calls the world, then it follows that the injunctions God gives to the Christian to be separate from the world and not polluted with it are of immediate relevance to the Christian's relation to the state. The believer then must make sure that he is not thus yoked together with unbelievers.

In spite of these conclusions, there are undoubtedly many functions of the state which stand open to the Christian's participation. This must especially be true of the modern democracy which has been strongly influenced by Christianity.

In this final part of the conclusion, the author asks indulgence to bring a wider general teaching of the New Testament into the observations. This is necessary to bring proper perspective to the problem and its conclusions. It has been evident that a large area of the obligation of the Christian to the state is that of praying for it and its functionaries. This is binding upon all Christians. They are to render willing obedience and subjection to the state in all moral and amoral situations. They must be disobedient only when compromise with sin is involved and when the commands of the state are immoral. This constitutes the Christian a good citizen of any state.

There are, however, a few other factors that must be voiced. Not only does the Christian benefit from the state, the state benefits greatly from the Christian. First, the Christians are the "salt" of the earth. As the preservative of society, the benefit which accrues to the state because of its Christian citizens is great. Second, the providential dealing of God, with especially the more moral and just state, on account of His children must also be significant.

But for the Christian to be the best citizen he must do the greatest possible good to his fellow men. This can be done only by the fulfillment of the great commission of Christ. To win men and women to Christ constitutes the very acme of good citizenship because to participate in redemption is the highest good of all. The Church in its obedience to its God-given task of proclaiming the gospel accomplishes this.

FOOTNOTES

[1]Reinhold Niebuhr, "A Communication: The Will of God and the Van Zeeland Report," *The Christian Century*, LV (Dec. 14, 1938), 1550.

BIBLIOGRAPHY

GENERAL BOOKS

Abrahams, Ray H. *Preachers Present Arms.* New York: Round Table Press, Inc., 1924,

Aulén, Gustav. *Church, Law and Society.* New York: Charles Scribner's Sons, 1948.

Barth, Karl. *Church and State.* Translated by G. Ronald Howe. London: Student Christian Movement Press, 1939.

Bettenson, Henry (ed.). *Documents of the Christian Church.* Oxford: University Press, 1943.

Bigg, Charles. *The Church's Task Under the Roman Empire.* Oxford: At the Clarendon Press, 1905.

Boettner, Loraine. *The Christian Attitude Toward War.* Grand Rapids: Wm. B. Eerdmans Publishing Co., 1942.

Broadbent, E. H. *The Pilgrim Church.* London: Pickering & Inglis, 1931.

Brunner, Emil. *The Divine Imperative.* Translated by Olive Wyon. Philadelphia: The Westminster Press, 1947.

——————. *Justice and the Social Order.* 1st ed. Translated by Mary Hottinger. New York: Harper & Brothers, 1945.

Cadman, S. Parkes. *Christianity and the State.* New York: The Macmillan Company, 1924.

Cadoux, John C. *The Early Christian Attitude to War.* London: Headley Bros. Publishers, Ltd., 1919.

——————. *The Early Church and the World.* Edinburgh: T. & T. Clark 1925.

——————. *Christian Pacifism Re-examined.* Oxford: Basil Blackwell, 1940.

Chafer, Lewis Sperry. *Systematic Theology.* Vol. VII. Dallas: Dallas Seminary Press, 1948.

Clark, Gordon H. *A Christian View of Men and Things.* Grand Rapids: Wm. B. Eerdmans Publishing Company, 1952.

Coates, J. R. *Bible Key Words from Gerhard Kittel's Theologisches Woerterbuch.* Translated and edited by J. R. Coates. New York: Harper & Brothers, Publishers, 1951.

Coker, Francis William. *Readings in Political Philosophy.* New York: The Macmillan Company, 1949.

Cullmann, Oscar. *Christ and Time.* Translated by Floyd V. Filson. London: SCM Press, Ltd., 1951.

Dawson, Christopher. *Religion and the Modern State.* New York: Sheed and Ward, 1940.

Ehrenstroem, Nils. *Christian Faith and the Modern State.* Translated by Denzil Patrick and Olive Wyon. Chicago: Willett, Clark & Company, 1937.

Garvie, Alfred E. *The Fatherly Rule of God.* New York: The Abingdon Press, 1935.

Gaussen, L. *Theopneustia*. Revised. Cincinnati: George S. Blanchard & Co., 1867.

Gavin, Frank. *Seven Centuries of the Problem of Church and State*. Princeton: Princeton University Press, 1938.

Gingerich, Melvin. *Service for Peace*. Akron: The Mennonite Central Committee, 1949.

Grubb, Kenneth G. (ed.) *The Church and the State*. "The Madras Series." Vol. VI. New York: International Missionary Council, 1939.

Hallesby, O. *Conscience*. Translated by Clarence J. Carlsen. 7th ed. Minneapolis: Augsburg Publishing House, 1938.

Halliday, W. R. *The Pagan Background of Early Christianity*. London: Hodder and Stoughton, Ltd., 1925.

Harnack, Adolf. *Militia Christi*. Tuebingen: Verlag von J. C. B. Mohr (Paul Siebeck), 1905.

Heering, G. J. *The Fall of Christianity*. Translated from Dutch by J. W. Thompson. London: George Allen & Unwin, Ltd., 1930.

Henry, Carl F. H. *The Protestant Dilemma*. Grand Rapids: Wm. B. Eerdmans, 1949.

Hershberger, Guy Franklin. *War, Peace, and Nonresistance*. Scottdale: The Herald Press, 1944.

Hutchinson, Paul. *The New Leviathan*. Chicago: Willett, Clark & Co., 1948.

Kirk, Walter W. van. *Religion Renounces War*. Chicago: Willett, Clark & Company, 1934.

Knudson, Albert C. *The Principles of Christian Ethics*. New York: Abingdon-Cokesbury Press, 1943.

Kuenneth, Walter, *Politik zwischen Daemon und Gott*. Berlin: Lutherisches Verlagshaus, 1954.

Laski, Harold J. *Authority in the Modern State*. New Haven: Yale University Press, 1927.

Lee, Umphrey. *The Historic Church and Modern Pacifism*. New York: Abingdon-Cokesbury Press, 1943.

Leiper, Henry Smith. *Christ's Way and the World's*. New York: The Abingdon Press, 1936.

Macgregor, G. H. C. *The New Testament Basis of Pacifism*. London: James Clarke & Co., Ltd., 1938.

Major, H. D. A., T. W. Manson, and C. J. Wright. *The Mission and Message of Jesus*. New York: E. P. Dutton and Co., Inc., 1947.

McNeill, John T. (ed.). *John Calvin on God and Political Duty*. New York: The Liberal Arts Press, 1950.

Neve, J. L. *A History of Christian Thought*. Vol. I. Philadelphia: The United Lutheran Publication House, 1943.

Newman, Albert Henry. *A Manual of Church History*. Vols. I, II. Revised and edited. Philadelphia. The American Baptist Publication Society, 1947.

Niebuhr, Reinhold. *An Interpretation of Christian Ethics*. New York: Harper & Brothers Publishers, 1935.

——————. *Christianity and Power Politics*. New York: Charles Scribner's Sons, 1940.

——————. *Christian Realism and Political Problems*. New York: Charles Scribner's Sons, 1953.

——————. *Moral Man and Immoral Society*. New York: Charles Scribner's Sons, 1941.

Oldham, J. G. *Church, Community and State*. New York: Harper & Brothers Publishers, 1935.

Orr, James (ed.), *et al*. *The International Standard Bible Encyclopedia*. Vols. II, IV. Grand Rapids: Wm. B. Eerdmans Publishing Co., 1949.

Osgniach, Augustine J. *The Christian State*. Milwaukee: The Bruce Publishing Company, 1943.

Pressencé, E. de. *Jesus Christ: His Times, Life and Work*. Translated by Annie Harwood-Holmden. London: Hodder and Stoughton, 1829.

Qualben, Lars P. *A History of the Christian Church*. Revised and enlarged. New York: Thomas Nelson and Sons, 1951.

Ramsay, W. M. *The Church in the Roman Empire*. London: G. P. Putnam's Sons, 1911.

——————. *The Letters to the Seven Churches of Asia*. New York: A. C. Armstrong & Sons, 1905.

Roberts, Alexander, and James Donaldson (eds.). *The Ante-Nicene Fathers*. Vol. IV. Buffalo: The Christian Publishing Company, 1885.

Rolston, Holmes. *The Social Message of the Apostle Paul*. Richmond: John Knox Press, 1942.

Rutenber, Culbert G. *The Dagger and the Cross*. New York: Fellowship Publications, 1950.

Sabine, George H. *A History of Political Theory*. New York: Henry Holt and Company, 1950.

Schaff, Philip. *History of the Christian Church*. Vols. I-III. Grand Rapids: Wm. B. Eerdmans Publishing Company, 1950.

Scott, Ernest F. *The Ethical Teaching of Jesus*. New York: The Macmillan Company, 1924.

Scott-Craig, T. S. K. *Christian Attitude to War and Peace*. New York: Charles Scribner's Sons, 1938.

Smith, C. Henry. *The Story of the Mennonites*, 3d ed. New Revision editor Cornelius Krahn. Newton: Mennonite Publishing Office, 1950.

Stokes, Anson Phelps. *Church and State in the United States*. Vol. I. New York: Harper & Brothers, Publishers, 1950.

Strong, August Hopkins. *Systematic Theology*. Philadelphia: Griffith & Rowland Press, 1909.

Tenney, Merrill C. *The New Testament: An Historical and Analytic Survey*. Grand Rapids: Wm. B. Eerdmans Publishing Company, 1953.

Terry, Milton S. *Biblical Hermeneutics*. Revised ed. New York: The Methodist Book Concern, 1911.

Thiessen, Henry Clarence. *Introduction to the New Testament.* Grand Rapids: Wm. B. Eerdmans Publishing Company, 1943.

Troeltsch, Ernst. *The Social Teaching of the Christian Churches.* Translated by Olive Wyon. 2 vols. New York: The Macmillan Company, 1931.

Unger, Merrill, F. *Biblical Demonology.* 2d. ed. Van Kempen Press, Inc., 1952.

Wallace, James. *Fundamentals of Christian Statesmanship.* New York: Fleming H. Revell Company, 1939.

Weiss, Bernhard. *Biblical Theology of the New Testament.* 3d. ed. Revised ed. Translated by David Eaton. Vol. I. Edinburgh: T. & T. Clark, 1882.

Wenger, John Christian. *Separated unto God.* Scottdale: Mennonite Publishing House, 1951.

Workman, Herbert Brook. *Persecutions in the Early Church.* London: H. H. Kelly, 1906.

BIBLE COMMENTARIES

Adeney, W. F. (ed.) *The Century Bible—St. Matthew.* Edinburgh: T. C. & E. C. Jack, Ltd., n. d.

Alford, Henry. *The Greek New Testament.* 3d. ed. Vol. I. New York: Harper & Brothers, Publishers, 1859.

Allen, Willoughby C. *A Critical and Exegetical Commentary of the Gospel According to St. Matthew.* New York: Charles Scribner's Sons, 1913.

Bernard, J. H. *A Critical and Exegetical Commentary on the Gospel According to St. John.* Edited by A. H. McNeile, "The International Critical Commentary." Vol. II. New York: Charles Scribner's Sons, 1929.

Bigg, Charles. *A Critical and Exegetical Commentary on the Epistles of St. Peter and St. Jude.* "The International Critical Commentary." Edinburgh: T. & T. Clark, 1901.

Bruce, F. F. *The Acts of the Apostles.* 2d ed. London: The Tyndale Press, 1952.

Cranfield, C. E. B. *The First Epistle of Peter.* London: SCM Press, Ltd. 1950.

Dodd, C. H. *The Epistle of Paul to the Romans.* "The Moffatt New Testament Commentary"; New York: Harper and Brothers, Publishers, 1932.

Godet, F. *Commentary on St. Paul's Epistle to the Romans.* Translated by A. Cusin. Revised and edited by Talbot W. Chambers. New York: Funk & Wagnalls, Publishers, 1883.

Hort, F. J. A. *The First Epistle of St. Peter*: I. 1—II. 17 London: Macmillan and Co., Ltd., 1898.

126

Hoskyns, Edwyn Clement. *The Fourth Gospel.* Edited by Francis Noel Davey. London: Faber and Faber, Ltd., 1947.

Hovey, Alvah, (ed.). *An American Commentary on the New Testament.* Vols. I, III, IV, VI. Philadelphia: American Baptist Publication Society, 1886.

Lange, J. P., and F. R. Fay. *Epistle of Paul to the Romans.* "A Commentary on the Holy Scriptures." Translated by J. F. Hurst. Revised and edited by P. Schaff and M. B. Riddle. New York: Charles Scribner's Sons, 1892.

——————. *The Gospel According to John.* "A Commentary on the Holy Scriptures." Translated, revised and edited by Philip Schaff. New York: Charles Scribner and Co., 1871.

Lenski, R. C. H. *The Interpretation of the Acts of the Apostles.* Columbus: Lutheran Book Concern, 1934.

——————. *The Interpretation of St. Paul's Epistle to the Romans.* Columbus: Lutheran Book Concern, 1936.

——————. *The Interpretation of the Epistles of St. Peter, St. John and St. Jude.* Columbus: Lutheran Book Concern, 1938.

Meyer, Heinrich August Wilhelm. *Critical and Exegetical Hand-Book to the Gospel of John.* Translated, revised and edited by Frederick Crombie. New York: Funk and Wagnalls Company, 1884.

——————. *Critical and Exegetical Hand-Book to the Gospel of Matthew.* Translated by Peter Christie. Edited and revised. New York: Funk & Wagnalls Company, 1884.

Moffatt, James. *The General Epistles.* "The Moffatt New Testament Commentary." New York: Harper and Brothers Publishers, n. d.

Nicoll, W. Robertson (ed.). *The Expositor's Greek New Testament.* Vol. I. London. Hodder and Stoughton, n. d.

Nygren, Anders. *Commentary on Romans.* Translated by Carl C. Rasmussen. Philadelphia: Muhlenberg Press, 1949.

Olshausen, Hermann. *Biblical Commentary on the New Testament.* Vol. I. Translated from 4th German ed. New York: Sheldon & Company Publishers, 1866.

Pieters, Albertus. *The Lamb, the Woman and the Dragon.* Grand Rapids: Zondervan Publishing House, 1937.

Plummer, Alfred. *A Critical and Exegetical Commentary of the Gospel According to St. Mark.* 10th ed. New York: Charles Scribner's Sons, 1914.

Robertson, Archibald Thomas. *Word Pictures in the New Testament.* Vols. I, IV, V, VI. New York: Harper and Brothers, 1930.

Sanday, William, and Arthur C. Headlam. *A Critical and Exegetical Commentary on the Epistle to the Romans.* New York: Charles Scribner's Sons, 1895.

Scott, E. F. *The Pastoral Epistles.* London: Hodder and Stoughton, 1948.

Selwyn, Edward Gordon. *The First Epistle of Peter.* London: Macmillan & Co., 1947.

Shedd, William G. T. *A Critical and Doctrinal Commentary upon the Epistle of St. Paul to the Romans.* New York: Charles Scribner's Sons, 1879.

Strack, Hermann, and Billerbeck, Paul. *Kommentar zum Neuen Testament aus Talmud und Midrasch.* Vols. I, III. Muenchen: C. H. Beck'sche Verlagsbuchhandlung, 1922-28.

Swete, Henry Barclay. *The Apocalypse of St. John.* 3d ed. London: Macmillan and Co., Ltd., 1909.

——————. *The Gospel According to Mark.* 3d. ed. London: Macmillan and Co., Ltd., 1909.

Windisch, Hans. *The Meaning of the Sermon on the Mount.* Translated by S. MacLean Gilmour. Philadelphia: The Westminster Press, 1937.

GREEK LANGUAGE BOOKS

The Englishman's Greek Concordance of the New Testament. 9th ed. London: Samuel Bagster and Sons (Limited), 1908.

A Greek-English Lexicon of the New Testament. Translated, revised and enlarged by Joseph Henry Thayer. New York: American Book Company, 1889.

Kittel, Gerhard (ed.). *Theologisches Woerterbuch zum Neuen Testament.* Vols. II, III. Stuttgart: Verlag von W. Kohlhammer, 1950.

Liddell, Henry George, and Robert Scott. *A Greek-English Lexicon.* Revised, edited. Oxford: At the Clarendon Press, n. d.

Robertson, A. T. *A Grammar of the Greek New Testament in the Light of Historical Research.* Nashville: Broadman Press, 1934.

ARTICLES

Bainton, Roland. "The Christian Century and the Christian and War," *The Christian Century,* LXI (May 3, 1944).

Bender, Harold S. "The Anabaptist Vision," *The Mennonite Quarterly Review,* XVIII (April, 1944).

Niebuhr, Reinhold. "A Communication: The Will of God and the Van Zeeland Report." *The Christian Century,* LV (Dec. 14, 1938).